Individual Serving

A FAVORITE RECIPE COLLECTION

OVER 200 RECIPES INCLUDING
APPETIZERS, BEVERAGES, DESSERTS AND MORE

Crescent Books
NEW YORK • AVENEL

A Balliett & Fitzgerald Book

This 1995 edition published by Crescent Books,
distributed by Random House Value Publishing, Inc.
40 Engelhard Avenue, Avenel, New Jersey 07001

Random House
New York • Toronto • London • Sydney • Auckland

A CIP catalog record for this book is available
from the Library of Congress.

ISBN
10 9 8 7 6 5 4 3 2 1

Printed in Malaysia

OCEAN SPRAY CRANBERRIES, INC.
Manager, Consumer Affairs: Linda Compton
Recipe Development Specialist/Food Stylist: Cynthia Taccini
Assistant Stylist: Diana Mordini
Corporate Archivist: Christine Hormell
Photography: Studio 3

Special thanks to John Groton, Bill Huelster,
Nancy Davis and Frank Calderon.

BALLIETT & FITZGERALD, INC.
Project Editor: Duncan Bock
Associate Editor: Susan Canavan
Production Artist: Dianna Russo
Editorial Assistants: Herb Ascherman and Tracy Liu

Book Design by Mary Tiegreen

CONTENTS

INTRODUCTION

THE SLENDER BLOSSOM OF THE CRANBERRY RESEMBLES THE HEAD OF A CRANE.

Even before their inspired pairing with turkey at the first Thanksgiving in 1621, cranberries were one of America's most characteristic fruits. In fact, the "bog ruby" is one of only three major fruits indigenous to North America (the others are the Concord grape and the blueberry).

Native Americans appreciated its versatility long before the Pilgrims landed on Plymouth Rock. They combined crushed cranberries, fat and ground venison to create pemmican, arguably America's first "convenience food," easily stored or transported on long journeys.

Native American women dyed their rugs and blankets with the colorful juice. Believing them to have medicinal, even mystical properties, medicine men boiled cranberry poultices to draw poison from arrow wounds.

As a symbol of goodwill, the cranberry also was used to heal differences. Disputes commonly were settled with a cranberry offering and the berries were consumed at peace feasts like that first Thanksgiving. The name of the powerful Delaware chief, Pakimintzen, came to mean "cranberry eater."

Nearly every tribe had a different name for the fruit, from the Cape Cod Wampanoags' and South Jersey Leni-Lenape's *ibimi* (bitter berry) to the Wisconsin Algonquins' *atoqua*. The Pilgrims first coined the term "crane-berry," as the gracefully arching, pale pink blossoms resembled the heads of cranes. Over time, "crane-berry" was contracted into its current name.

The new settlers also valued the multi-faceted fruit. Every autumn, families gathered to pick enough wild berries to last through the winter. They were considered so vital that in 1773, anyone on Cape Cod caught picking more than a quart before September 20th—more than a month before peak harvest—was subject to a $1 fine.

Pilgrim women adopted the cranberry for use in tarts and preserves. *The Pilgrim Cookbook* appeared in 1663 describing cranberry sauce and the 1683 *Compleat Cook's Guide* included a recipe for the first cranberry juice cocktail!

Colonists also appreciated the fruit's decorative appeal. Dresses, petticoats and quilts, dyed crimson with the juice, fetched high prices, while strings of bright berries festooned Christmas trees. Sailors ate cranberries to prevent scurvy. We now know that the berries are a source of Vitamin C.

*IN FLOODED BOGS, WORKERS RAKE AND CORRAL THE FLOATING BERRIES
AFTER THEY HAVE BEEN CHURNED LOOSE FROM THEIR VINES.*

Taking another cue from their Native American neighbors, New Englanders also used them to preserve the peace. In 1677, after they had defied the law and minted their own Pine Tree shillings, the Puritans shipped their three choicest products to England as a gift to appease King Charles II's wrath: two hogsheads of samp (boiled and broken Indian corn), three thousand salted codfish and 10 barrels of cranberries. In 1787, when James Madison wanted background information from Thomas Jefferson, then in France, to help draft the Constitution, Jefferson requested a gift of apples, pecans and cranberries in return.

Despite their bold, assertive flavor, cranberries are rather fragile, thriving only in a sophisticated wetlands system. They require acid peat soil, abundant fresh water and a prolonged growing season from April to November to reach maturity.

The wild berry finally was tamed in 1816. Captain Henry Hall of Dennis, Cape Cod, noted that cranberries grew fatter and juicier where sand from nearby dunes blew over the vines. He transplanted some vines to his low, swampy ground, covering the shoots with a layer of sand. This began the process of cultivation.

Hall's venture soon was imitated everywhere the berry grew wild, from Massachusetts to Rhode Island, New Jersey, Wisconsin, Washington and Oregon. These six states, along with Canadian Nova Scotia, Ontario, Quebec and British Columbia, comprise the chief cranberry-growing areas in North America.

The next advance occurred in the 1880s when a New Jersey grower named John "Peg Leg" Webb discovered the "cranberry bounce." Being one-legged, he couldn't carry his crop down from the storage loft of his barn. Instead he poured it down the steps.

Only the firmest fruit bounced to the bottom; rotten or bruised berries remained on the steps. This led to the invention of bounceboards.

Even today, cranberry processors in New England give the berries seven chances to bounce over four-inch barriers. Any that don't display the distinctive springiness are rejected.

Popular misconception suggests that the cranberry grows in water. Actually, it grows on vines in bogs or marshes: beds layered with sand, peat, gravel and clay. For more than 100 years, cranberries were combed laboriously from the vines with wooden hand scoops.

BOTTOM: FOR MORE THAN A CENTURY, CRANBERRIES WERE HARVESTED BY HAND WITH WOODEN SCOOPS. (SCOOP, CIRCA 1924) TOP: WORKERS PUSHED THE SCOOPS BEFORE THEM, GENTLY ROCKING THEM SO THEIR WOODEN TEETH COMBED THE VINES AND LIFTED OFF THE BERRIES. RIGHT: A FAMILY OF GATHERERS, CIRCA 1890. BOTTOM RIGHT: BY THE MID-1920S CRANBERRY BOXES HAD COMPLETELY REPLACED BARRELS FOR SHIPPING AS WELL AS STORAGE ON THE BOGS.

Today, cranberries are harvested primarily by two methods. In dry harvesting, growers use mechanical pickers resembling giant lawnmowers. Their moving teeth gently comb the berries from the vines. These berries commonly are sold fresh for cooking and baking.

In wet harvesting, growers flood the bogs with water. They use reels, nicknamed "eggbeaters," to churn the water and dislodge the cranberries. The fruit floats to the surface, where they are raked and corralled. Wet harvested berries are used primarily in juice drinks and sauces.

Perhaps because the wetlands are a delicately balanced ecosystem, growers are in the forefront of conservation. They are masters of water man-

agement and careful stewards of the environment. It is common to recycle water to reservoirs and other bogs, while sophisticated irrigation systems filter groundwater, recharge aquifers and control floods by retaining storm runoff.

The cranberry was considered a seasonal fruit until an enterprising lawyer-turned-grower named Marcus L. Urann realized that the berries he harvested exceeded demand. Urann hated to see good fruit go to waste, so he perfected a tasty sauce that he canned and called Ocean Spray in 1912.

A true visionary and pioneer, Urann recognized that canned, frozen and processed foods were the wave of the future. Fellow growers resisted at first, but led by its canning division,

Urann's Cape Cod Cranberry Company grew rapidly over the next two decades.

Two other cranberry pioneers, John Makepeace, president of the A.D. Makepeace Company of Wareham, Massachusetts, and Elizabeth Lee, president of the Cranberry Products Company of New Egypt, New Jersey, rapidly followed Urann's lead. In 1930, the three growers were competing for the East Coast market when Urann suggested they merge to form a cranberry growers' cooperative.

The often-contentious negotiations ended when Urann agreed to transfer the lucrative Ocean Spray name and trademark to the new Cooperative. Under the name Cranberry Canners, Inc., the merger was approved on August 14, 1930.

It was somehow appropriate that a cooperative like Ocean Spray originated in the Northeast, where so many 19th century reform movements and Utopian communities were founded. From the start, Ocean Spray was democratic and progressive. Finns, Cape Verdeans and Jamaicans were among the many ethnic groups that contributed to the cranberry industry as farmers, laborers and managers.

In 1934 the New England Cranberry Sales

ABOVE: JANET TAYLOR AND KIM BOSWORTH OF THE NATIONAL CRANBERRY ASSOCIATION'S HOME ECONOMICS DEPARTMENT PREPARED ONE OF THEIR DISHES FOR A PUBLICITY SHOT. BELOW: RECIPE BOOKS FROM THE OCEAN SPRAY COLLECTION.

Company growers joined the Cooperative and their New Jersey counterparts followed suit in 1938. The member growers of the Wisconsin Sales Company voted unanimously to join Ocean Spray in 1940. When Washington and Oregon growers followed the next year, Ocean Spray became a national cooperative.

Ocean Spray also was adding cranberry products. Cranberry juice cocktail made its first appearance in the early 1930s. Ads praised it as "a pleasant, smooth drink with delicious flavor and sure relief from faintness, exhaustion, and thirst. A glass when retiring promotes sleep and a clean mouth in the morning—even to the smoker."

In the early 1940s, Dehydrated Cranberries (to supply the Armed Forces) and Cranberry-Orange Marmalade were marketed.

Ocean Spray created its famous Test Kitchen, located in Hanson, Massachusetts, in 1939 as part of a drive to increase consumer awareness and expand the cranberry's seasonality. Janet Taylor, then Ocean Spray's director of home economics, developed cranberry recipes.

She published them with decorating tips and fun facts in the Cranberry Kitchen newsletter, which was sent to home economists nationwide. Famous women—including Ruth Wakefield, owner of the renowned Toll House restaurant, flamboyant actress (and grower) Gertrude Lawrence and the Honorable Margaret Chase Smith, U.S. Senator from Maine—were asked to contribute their favorite cranberry recipes.

Ocean Spray has continued to experiment with new recipes, helping to adapt the all-American cranberry to dishes as varied and delicious as fajitas and fruited brie bake. Using fruit juices from guava to grapefruit (a group of citrus

THE AMERICAN CRANBERRY EXCHANGE INTRODUCED THE EATMOR LABELS AROUND 1916, GROUPING BERRIES UNDER VARIOUS BRAND NAMES LIKE HOLIDAY.

growers joined the Cooperative in 1976), Ocean Spray's recipes draw on worldwide cuisines. almost any foodstuff.

The cranberry always has been a staple of New England cooking, but it's fitting that this indigenous fruit adapts beautifully to other classic American cuisines, from Southern to Southwestern. Regional favorites like pecan breaded pork, country-style ribs and even chili are practically reinvented with the addition of cranberries.

Today, Cindy Taccini, head of Ocean Spray's Test Kitchen, always is surprised by the berry's versatility. Many cooks may think its inimitable sassy flavor only lends itself to turkey, muffins and perhaps cranberry orange relish. But cranberries can enhance every aspect of the meal, from breads and beverages to appetizers, salads, main courses and, of course, desserts.

The tangy berry complements an astonishing range of sweet and sour tastes, including chocolate, maple, mustard, even jalapeño! The secret lies in its sharp flavor, which can stand up to

The visual appeal of cooking with cranberries is an added bonus: that rich deep crimson, lightened to a warm pink in cream-based sauces, provides a feast for the eye as well as the palate. All the more reason to regard the "bog ruby" as a national treasure.

CHAPTER 1

THE CLASSICS

CRANBERRRY NUT PIE

1 1/4 cups OCEAN SPRAY® fresh or frozen
   cranberries
1/4 cup brown sugar
1/4 cup chopped walnuts
1 egg
1/2 cup sugar
1/2 cup all-purpose flour
1/3 cup butter or margarine, melted
Vanilla ice cream

Preheat oven to 325 degrees. Butter a 9-inch
pie plate.

Layer cranberries on bottom of pan. Sprinkle
with brown sugar and nuts. In a bowl, beat egg
until thick; gradually add sugar, beating
until thoroughly blended. Stir in
flour and melted butter;
blend well. Pour over
cranberries.

Bake 45 minutes.
Cut in wedges.
Serve with ice
cream. Makes 6
servings.

CRANBERRY APPLE CRISP

5 cups sliced tart apples (about 6 medium apples)
1 1/2 cups OCEAN SPRAY® fresh or frozen
   cranberries
1/3 cup granulated sugar
1/2 cup all purpose flour
1/2 cup brown sugar
1 teaspoon cinnamon
1/4 cup butter or margarine

Preheat oven to 375 degrees. Lightly grease a 9-
inch square baking pan.

Pare and core apples. Layer apples and cranberries in pan sprinkling with granulated sugar as
you layer. Mix together flour, brown sugar, and
cinnamon. Work in butter until mixture
is light and crumbly. Sprinkle topping evenly over apples and
cranberries.

Bake 45 minutes
or until apples are
tender. Makes 9
servings.

*PRECEDING: CRANBERRY APPLE CRISP. ABOVE: AN INSPIRATION TO NEW ENGLAND GROWERS LIKE
OCEAN SPRAY'S MARCUS L. URANN, THE WISCONSIN CRANBERRY SALES COMPANY WAS THE FIRST
CRANBERRY MARKETING COOPERATIVE, FORMED IN 1905.*

FROZEN CRANBERRY CREAM PIE

2 3-ounce packages cream cheese, softened
1 16-ounce can OCEAN SPRAY® jellied
   cranberry sauce
1/2 teaspoon vanilla
1 teaspoon grated lemon peel
2 cups frozen non-dairy whipped topping, thawed
1 baked 9-inch pie shell

Beat the softened cream cheese until fluffy in a small mixing bowl. Add cranberry sauce, vanilla, and lemon peel, beating until smooth and creamy. Gently stir in whipped topping. Spoon into baked pie shell. Freeze until firm, about 4 hours. When ready to serve, allow to stand at room temperature 15 minutes before cutting. Makes 6–8 servings.

APPLE PIE A LA ZING

4 cups pared, sliced apples
2 cups OCEAN SPRAY® fresh or frozen
   cranberries
3/4 cup brown sugar
1/2 cup sugar
1/3 cup flour
1 teaspoon cinnamon
3/4 cup chopped walnuts, optional
Pastry for a 9-inch two crust pie

Preheat oven to 425 degrees.
Combine all ingredients, except pastry, in a medium mixing bowl; mix well. Pour into a pastry-lined pie plate. Cover with top crust. Seal edges, and cut several slits in top crust.

Bake 50 minutes or until golden brown. Cover edges with foil if they begin to brown too quickly. Makes 1 pie.

FRESH CRANBERRY ORANGE RELISH

1 12-ounce package OCEAN SPRAY® fresh or
   frozen cranberries
1 medium orange
3/4 to 1 cup sugar

Slice unpeeled orange into eighths; remove seeds. Place half the cranberries and half the orange slices in food processor container. Process until mixture is evenly chopped. Transfer to a bowl. Repeat with remaining cranberries and orange slices. Stir in sugar. Makes about 3 cups.

NOTE: May also be prepared in a food grinder.

*CRANBERRY ORANGE RELISH
HAS BEEN POPULAR FOR
GENERATIONS.*

No Cooking!
CRANBERRY ORANGE RELISH
Put through *food chopper:*
   1 lb. Ocean Spray fresh cranberries
   (4 cups).
   2 oranges (including rind and pulp).
   Stir in 2 cups sugar.
   Store in refrigerator several hours
   so flavors will blend.
Makes 2 pints.
Keeps for weeks, if refrigerated.
How to serve:
   Delicious with any meat;
   chicken, turkey, ham, or
   cold cuts.
Serve with cottage cheese
   for a delicious salad.
Fold one cup relish into raspberry gelatin just as it
   begins to jell. Makes
   delicious molded salad.

CRANBERRY MOUSSE

1 cup OCEAN SPRAY® cranberry juice cocktail
1 3-ounce package raspberry flavored gelatin
1 16-ounce can OCEAN SPRAY® jellied
   cranberry sauce
2 cups frozen non-dairy whipped topping, thawed

Heat cranberry juice cocktail to boiling in a saucepan. Remove from heat. Stir in raspberry gelatin until dissolved. Using an electric mixer on high speed, beat cranberry sauce in a small bowl for one minute. Stir into gelatin mixture. Chill until it begins to thicken, but not set. Gently mix in whipped topping, using a rubber scraper. Spoon into serving dishes or pie shell. Chill until firm. Makes 8 servings.

HOMEMADE JELLIED CRANBERRY SAUCE

1 cup sugar
1 cup water
1 12-ounce package OCEAN SPRAY® fresh
   or frozen cranberries

Combine sugar and water in a medium saucepan. Bring to a boil; add cranberries, return to a boil. Reduce heat and boil gently for 10 minutes, stirring occasionally.

   Place a wire mesh strainer over a medium mixing bowl. Pour contents of saucepan into strainer. Press cranberries with the back of a spoon, frequently scraping the outside of the strainer, until no pulp is left.

   Stir contents of bowl. Pour into serving container. Cover and cool completely at room temperature. Refrigerate until serving time. Makes 1 cup.

CRANBERRY ORANGE FRUIT DIP

1 cup vanilla yogurt
2/3 cup CRAN•FRUIT® cranberry orange
   crushed fruit
1/2 teaspoon fresh grated lemon peel
1/4 teaspoon lemon juice

Mix together yogurt, crushed fruit, lemon peel, and lemon juice in a small mixing bowl. Chill. Prepare fruits, such as apple wedges, melon balls, pineapple chunks, orange sections, banana slices or grapes, for dipping. Makes 1 2/3 cups.

CRANBERRY NUT BREAD

2 cups all-purpose flour
1 cup sugar
1 1/2 teaspoons baking powder
1 teaspoon salt
1/2 teaspoon baking soda
3/4 cup orange juice
1 tablespoon grated orange peel
2 tablespoons shortening
1 egg, well beaten
1 1/2 cups OCEAN SPRAY® fresh or frozen
   cranberries, coarsely chopped
1/2 cup chopped nuts

Preheat oven to 350 degrees. Grease a 9 x 5-inch loaf pan.

   Mix together flour, sugar, baking powder, salt and baking soda in a medium mixing bowl. Stir in orange juice, orange peel, shortening and egg. Mix until well blended. Stir in cranberries and nuts. Turn into pan.

   Bake for 55 minutes or until toothpick inserted in center comes out clean. Cool on a rack 15 minutes; remove from pan. Makes 1 loaf.

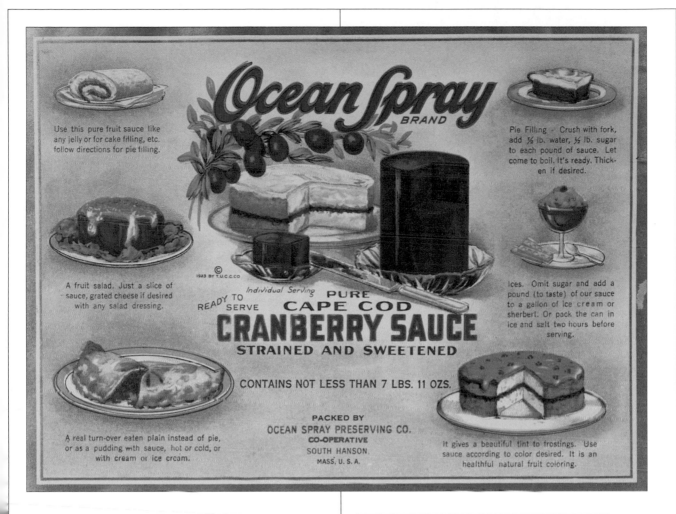

LABEL FOR A 7-POUND, 11-OUNCE "HOTEL SIZE" CAN. THIS EXAMPLE DATES TO 1929.

Fresh Cranberry Sauce

- 1 **cup water**
- 1 **cup granulated sugar**
- 1 **12-ounce package OCEAN SPRAY® fresh or frozen cranberries**

Combine water and sugar in a medium saucepan. Bring to boil; add cranberries, return to boil. Reduce heat and boil gently for 10 minutes, stirring occasionally. Pour into a medium glass mixing bowl. Cover and cool completely at room temperature. Refrigerate until serving time. Makes 2 1/4 cups.

*"A cranberry a day
keeps you feeling okay all the
live long day.
That's what I say."*

—Mark Twain

*THE PRESENTATION OF TURKEY AND CRANBERRIES TO PRESIDENT EISENHOWER FOR HIS FIRST
THANKSGIVING DINNER IN THE WHITE HOUSE MADE A LASTING IMPRESSION.
MISS ELLEN STILLMAN, VICE PRESIDENT, ADVERTISING, IS SHOWN WITH A BASKET OF
CRANBERRIES, GIFT OF THE NATIONAL CRANBERRY ASSOCIATION.*

CRANBERRY BUTTER

1 cup butter, softened
1 cup OCEAN SPRAY® jellied or whole berry
   cranberry sauce
Pecans, chopped (optional)

Whip butter in a medium mixing bowl until light
and fluffy, using an electric mixer on high speed.
Add cranberry sauce and mix on medium speed
until thoroughly combined.

Place in individual or large serving container.
Sprinkle with pecans, if desired. Best when served
at room temperature. Serve with muffins, bagels,
pancakes, etc. Makes 2 cups.

CRANBERRY FRUIT STUFFING

1 cup OCEAN SPRAY® fresh or frozen cranberries
1 cup pineapple chunks, cut in half, reserving
   1/2 cup juice
1 cup mandarin oranges, drained
1 cup golden raisins
1/2 cup slivered almonds
6 slices stale bread, torn into small pieces

Preheat oven to 350 degrees.

Combine all ingredients in a medium mixing
bowl. Add 1/2 cup reserved pineapple juice;
mix well.

Bake stuffing in a covered casserole dish for
45 minutes or until stuffing is heated through.
Makes about 4 cups.

FROZEN CRANBERRY MARGARITA

5 ounces OCEAN SPRAY® whole berry
   cranberry sauce
1 1/2 ounces white tequila
1 1/2 ounces lime juice
1/2 ounce triple sec
5 ounces crushed ice
Strawberry fan, garnish

Put all ingredients, except garnish, in a blender.
Blend for a few seconds on high speed or until ingredients are thoroughly combined. Pour into a large
glass. Garnish with a strawberry fan. Makes 1 serving.

FROZEN CRANBERRY DAIQUIRI

6 ounces OCEAN SPRAY® jellied cranberry sauce
2 ounces rum
1/4 ounce lime juice
8 ounces crushed ice
Whipped cream, garnish

Put all ingredients, except garnish, in a
blender. Blend for a few seconds on high
speed or until ingredients are thoroughly
combined. Pour into a large glass. Garnish
with whipped cream. Makes 1 serving.

CAPE CODDER

3 ounces OCEAN SPRAY® cranberry juice
   cocktail, chilled
1 1/2 ounces vodka
1 teaspoon lemon juice

Pour into a tall glass with ice. Makes 1 serving.

SEA BREEZE

3 ounces OCEAN SPRAY® cranberry juice
   cocktail, chilled
3 ounces OCEAN SPRAY® grapefruit
   juice, chilled
1 1/2 ounces vodka

Pour into a tall glass with ice. Makes 1 serving.

MADRAS

3 ounces OCEAN SPRAY® cranberry juice
   cocktail chilled
1 1/2 ounces orange juice, chilled
1/2 ounce vodka

Pour into a tall glass with ice.
Makes 1 serving.

*LEFT TO RIGHT: MADRAS,
FROZEN CRANBERRY
DAIQUIRI.*

CHAPTER 2

DRINKS WITH A PUNCH

Ocean Spray BRAND

1 QUART   NET

CRANBERRY JUICE
COCKTAIL
MADE FROM
Selected Vine Ripened Cranberries cooked where grown. No artificial
coloring, flavor or preservative added. Mild, tart, delicious flavor, leaving
a cool, pleasant mouth. Serve 3 oz. portion as an appetizer, or larger
glass with meals. Serve chilled.
CRANBERRY CANNERS, Inc.
South Hanson, Massachusetts

PINK WITH A TWIST

6 ounces OCEAN SPRAY® pink
grapefruit juice cocktail
1 1/2 ounces rum
2 ounces lemon-lime soda
Lemon twist, garnish

Pour all ingredients, except garnish, into a tall glass with ice. Garnish with a lemon twist. Makes 1 serving.

TROPICAL PINK

4 ounces OCEAN SPRAY® pink
grapefruit juice cocktail
1 ounce coconut-flavored rum
Orange slice, garnish

Pour all ingredients, except garnish, into a glass with ice. Garnish with an orange slice. Makes 1 serving.

HULA HOOP

3 ounces OCEAN SPRAY® pink
grapefruit juice cocktail
1 ounce vodka
Orange slice, garnish

Pour all ingredients, except garnish, into a short glass with ice. Garnish with orange slice. Makes 1 serving.

PRECEDING: (CLOCKWISE) CRANBERRY MAI TAI, LUNAR 9, KOKOMO, TROPICAL PINK AND PIRATE'S PASSION (PAGE 27).

HOLLERIN' REBEL

8 ounces OCEAN SPRAY® pink
grapefruit juice cocktail
1 ounce Southern Comfort
Jalapeño pepper, garnish

Pour all ingredients, except garnish, into a glass with ice. Garnish with a jalapeño pepper. Makes 1 serving.

PINK PANTHER

4 ounces OCEAN SPRAY® pink
grapefruit juice cocktail
1 1/2 ounces rum
2 ounces club soda or raspberry
ginger ale
Cherry, garnish

Pour pink grapefruit juice cocktail and rum into a tall glass with ice. Top with club soda or raspberry ginger ale. Garnish with a cherry. Makes 1 serving.

KOKOMO

3 ounces MAUNA LA'I®
ISLAND GUAVA™ Hawaiian
guava juice drink
1 1/2 ounces tropical schnapps
Strawberry or cherry, garnish

Pour all ingredients, except for garnish, into a glass with crushed ice. Garnish with a strawberry or cherry. Makes 1 serving.

RED DEVIL

4 ounces OCEAN SPRAY® Ruby
Red grapefruit juice drink
1 ounce Southern Comfort
Club soda
Lemon or lime wedge, garnish

Pour grapefruit juice drink and Southern Comfort into a glass filled with ice. Top with a splash of club soda. Garnish with a lemon or lime wedge. Makes 1 serving.

SUNSET BLUES

4 ounces OCEAN SPRAY® Ruby
Red grapefruit juice drink
1 ounce pineapple juice
1 ounce light rum
1/2 ounce triple sec
1/2 ounce lime juice
Paper umbrella, garnish
Pineapple wedge, garnish

Pour all ingredients, except garnishes, into a glass with crushed ice. Garnish with a paper umbrella and a pineapple wedge. Makes 1 serving.

RED DOG

3 ounces OCEAN SPRAY® Ruby
Red grapefruit juice drink
3/4 ounce citrus flavored
vodka

Pour all ingredients into a short glass with ice. Makes 1 serving.

LUNAR 9

8 ounces OCEAN SPRAY® Ruby
Red grapefruit juice drink
3/4 ounce blue curaçao

Pour all ingredients into a glass
with ice. Makes 1 serving.

OFF THE WALLABIE

6 ounces OCEAN SPRAY®
grapefruit juice
2 ounces pineapple juice
1 ounce raspberry liqueur
1/2 ounce Southern Comfort
1/2 teaspoon grenadine

Pour all ingredients into a glass
with ice. Stir well. Makes 1
serving.

CRANBERRY MAI TAI

4 ounces OCEAN SPRAY®
cranberry juice cocktail
1 ounce pineapple juice
1 ounce rum
1/2 ounce triple sec
1/2 ounce lime juice
Pineapple slice, garnish
Orange slice, garnish
Cherry, garnish

Pour all ingredients, except garnishes, into a glass with ice.
Garnish with a pineapple slice,
orange slice and a cherry.
Makes 1 serving.

*CRANBERRY COCKTAIL WAS FIRST BOTTLED IN THE 1930s UNDER THE OCEAN SPRAY
BRAND NAME.*

KENTUCKY COOLER

4 ounces OCEAN SPRAY®
cranberry juice cocktail
4 ounces unsweetened iced tea
1 1/2 ounces peach-flavored
whiskey
Mint leaf, garnish

Pour all ingredients, except for
garnish, into a glass with ice.
Garnish with a mint leaf. Makes
1 serving.

SYDNEY SIDER

8 ounces OCEAN SPRAY®
cranberry juice cocktail
1/2 ounce spiced rum
1/2 ounce cinnamon schnapps
Whipped cream, garnish
Dash cinnamon, garnish

Heat all ingredients, except garnishes, in a saucepan or
microwave. Pour into a mug.
Garnish with whipped cream
and a dash of cinnamon. Makes
1 serving.

SNOW BLOWER

6 ounces CRANAPPLE®
   cranberry apple juice drink
1 teaspoon lemon juice
Pinch cloves or nutmeg
1 ounce rum, optional
Lemon slice, garnish

Heat cranberry apple drink,
lemon juice and cloves or nutmeg in a small saucepan. Pour
into a mug and stir in rum, if
desired. Garnish with a lemon
slice. Makes 1 serving.

CINNAMON SNAP

4 ounces OCEAN SPRAY®
   cranberry juice cocktail
1 ounce Southern Comfort
3/4 ounce cinnamon schnapps

Heat all ingredients in a small
saucepan. Pour into a mug.
Makes 1 serving.

ABORIGINAL SPIRIT

8 ounces OCEAN SPRAY®
   cranberry juice cocktail
1/2 ounce almond liqueur
1/2 ounce coffee brandy

Heat all ingredients in a
saucepan or microwave. Pour
into a mug. Makes 1 serving

*HOT CRANBERRY DRINKS: (LEFT TO
RIGHT) SNOW BLOWER, CINNAMON
SNAP AND ABORIGINAL SPIRIT.*

EAST END LIGHTS

6 ounces CRAN•CHERRY™
   cherry cranberry juice drink
1/2 ounce blue curaçao
1/2 ounce triple sec

Pour all ingredients into a glass
with ice. Makes 1 serving.

SWEET INDULGENCE

6 ounces CRAN•CHERRY™
   cherry cranberry juice drink
1 1/2 ounces coffee-flavored
   liqueur
1/3 cup chocolate ice cream

Put all ingredients in a blender.
Blend for a few seconds on high
speed or until ingredients are
thoroughly combined. Makes 1
serving

CRANBERRY SPRITZER

3 ounces CRANAPPLE®
   cranberry apple juice drink,
   chilled
1 1/2 ounces white wine, chilled
Club soda, chilled

Pour cranberry apple drink and
wine into a large wine glass
with ice. Top with a splash of
club soda. Makes 1 serving.

PIRATE'S PASSION

3 ounces OCEAN SPRAY®
   grapefruit juice
1 1/2 ounces lemon flavored
   vodka

Pour ingredients into a glass
with ice. Makes 1 serving.

CRANBERRY SANGRIA

1 48-ounce bottle OCEAN
   SPRAY® cranberry juice
   cocktail
3 cups sweet red wine
1 orange, sliced
1 lemon, sliced
Sugar to taste

Mix cranberry juice cocktail, wine
and sliced fruits in a large pitcher. Sweeten to taste. Chill several
hours to blend flavors. Serve with
fruit in large wine glasses. Makes
18 4-ounce servings.

BAT BITE

6 ounces OCEAN SPRAY®
   cranberry juice cocktail
1 1/2 ounces black rum
Lime wedge, garnish

Pour ingredients, except garnish, into a large glass with ice.
Garnish with lime wedge. Makes
1 serving.

HOT BUTTERED CRANBERRY

**8 ounces OCEAN SPRAY®
cranberry juice cocktail or
CRANAPPLE® cranberry
apple juice drink
1 piece stick cinnamon
3 teaspoons brown sugar
Dash ground cinnamon
2 teaspoons butter
2 tablespoons gold rum**

Heat cranberry juice cocktail or
cranberry apple drink and cinnamon stick in small saucepan.
Put brown sugar, ground cinnamon, butter and rum in a mug.
Pour hot cranberry mixture into
the mug. Stir gently before
serving. Makes 1 serving.

HOT SPICED TODDY

**1 cup CITRUS REFRESHERS™
citrus peach juice drink
1 cinnamon stick
Dash ground cinnamon
3 teaspoons brown sugar
2 teaspoons butter, optional
1 ounce black rum**

Heat citrus peach juice drink
and cinnamon stick in a small
saucepan. Put ground cinnamon, brown sugar, butter and
rum in a mug. Pour hot citrus
peach juice drink into the mug.
Stir gently before serving.
Garnish with a cinnamon stick.
Makes 1 serving.

MIMSY

**5 ounces OCEAN SPRAY®
cranberry juice cocktail
5 ounces dry champagne, chilled**

Pour ingredients into a champagne flute. Makes 1 serving.

A KEY TO NEW DRINKS

made with **Ocean Spray**
Cranberry Juice Cocktail

RECIPE BROCHURE, CIRCA 1960S.

CROCODILE ROCKER

**7 ounces OCEAN SPRAY®
grapefruit juice
2 ounces orange juice
1 1/2 ounces blue curaçao**

Pour all ingredients into a glass
with ice. Makes 1 serving.

BATHTUB GIN LEMONADE

**8 ounces OCEAN SPRAY®
cranberry juice cocktail
4 ounces lemonade
1 1/2 ounces gin
Lemon slice, garnish**

Pour all ingredients, except
garnish, into a large glass with
ice. Garnish with a lemon slice.
Makes 1 serving.

SOUR PUSS

**7 ounces OCEAN SPRAY® Ruby
Red grapefruit juice drink
2 ounces liquid whiskey
sour mix
1 1/2 ounces lemon-flavored
vodka**

Pour all ingredients into a large
glass with ice. Makes 1 serving.

RECKLESS RICKSHAW

**5 ounces MAUNA LA'I®
¡MANGO-MANGO!™
Hawaiian guava juice drink
2 ounces orange juice
2 ounces vodka**

Pour all ingredients into a glass
with ice. Makes 1 serving.

CRANBERRY SUNRISE

3 ounces CRAN•RASPBERRY®
  raspberry cranberry juice
  drink
1 ounce gold tequila
1/2 ounce pineapple juice
Pineapple slice, garnish

Pour all ingredients, except garnish, into a shaker half-filled with ice. Shake well. Strain into a glass. Garnish with pineapple slice. Makes 1 serving.

MAD HATTER

3 ounces CRAN•RASPBERRY®
  raspberry cranberry juice
  drink
1 1/2 ounces vodka
1/2 ounce orange juice

Pour all ingredients into a glass with ice. Makes 1 serving.

LOUISIANA LEMONADE

4 ounces OCEAN SPRAY®
  cranberry juice cocktail
4 ounces lemonade
1 1/2 ounces peach-flavored
  whiskey
Lemon slice, garnish

Pour all ingredients, except garnish, into a glass with ice. Garnish with lemon slice. Makes 1 serving.

MOLOAA BEACH

3 ounces MAUNA LA'I®
  PARADISE PASSION™
  Hawaiian guava passion juice
  drink
3 ounces pineapple juice
1/2 ounce rum

Pour all ingredients into a glass with ice. Makes 1 serving.

CARIBBEAN CRUISE

4 ounces MAUNA LA'I®
  ISLAND GUAVA™ Hawaiian
  guava juice drink
1 1/2 ounces coconut-flavored
  rum
Pineapple slice, garnish

Pour ingredients, except garnish, into a glass with ice. Garnish with pineapple slice. Makes 1 serving.

HAWAIIAN SANGRIA

3 ounces MAUNA LA'I®
  ISLAND GUAVA™ Hawaiian
  guava juice drink
3 ounces white zinfandel wine
Dash brandy
Strawberry or cherry, garnish

Pour all ingredients, except garnish, into a glass with ice. Garnish with strawberry or cherry. Makes 1 serving.

KALIHIWAI

3 ounces MAUNA LA'I®
  PARADISE PASSION™
  Hawaiian guava passion
  juice drink, chilled
1/2 ounce peach schnapps

Pour ingredients into a glass with ice. Makes 1 serving.

TOP HAT

6 ounces CITRUS REFRESH-
  ERS™ citrus orange juice
  drink
1 1/2 ounces coffee flavored
  liqueur

Pour ingredients into a glass with ice. Makes 1 serving.

KOALA KOOLER

9 ounces OCEAN SPRAY®
  cranberry juice cocktail
1 ounce coffee liqueur
1/2 ounce chocolate liqueur

Pour all ingredients into a glass with ice. Makes 1 serving.

TUMBLEWEED

6 ounces CITRUS REFRESH-
  ERS™ citrus orange juice
  drink
1 1/2 ounces Southern Comfort

Pour ingredients into a glass with ice. Makes 1 serving.

PEACH FUZZ

6 ounces CITRUS REFRESH-
ERS™ citrus peach juice
drink
3/4 ounce peach schnapps
1/2 ounce vodka
Lime twist, garnish

Pour all ingredients, except
garnish, into a glass with ice.
Garnish with lime twist.
Makes 1 serving.

SEA MIST

6 ounces CITRUS REFRESH-
ERS™ citrus cranberry
juice drink
1 1/4 ounces vodka
Lemon slice, garnish

Pour all ingredients, except
garnish, into a glass with ice.
Garnish with lemon slice.
Makes 1 serving.

DRAGON'S TAIL

8 ounces OCEAN SPRAY® Ruby
Red grapefruit juice drink
1 1/4 ounces tropical schnapps
Pineapple wedge, garnish
Cherry, garnish

Pour all ingredients, except garnish, into a glass with ice.
Garnish with pineapple wedge
and cherry. Makes 1 serving.

FUNKY MONKEY

8 ounces OCEAN SPRAY®
cranberry juice cocktail or
CRAN•RASPBERRY®
raspberry cranberry juice
drink
2 ounces half-and-half
1 ounce raspberry liqueur
1 ounce chocolate syrup
Whipped cream, garnish
Chocolate sprinkles, garnish
Maraschino cherry, garnish

Put all ingredients, except garnishes, in a blender. Blend on
high speed for a few seconds or
until ingredients are thoroughly
combined. Pour into a tall glass.
Garnish with whipped cream,
chocolate sprinkles and cherry.
Makes 1 serving.

PEACH PARADISE

6 ounces CITRUS REFRESH-
ERS™ citrus orange juice
drink
1 1/2 ounces peach schnapps
1/2 ounce vodka
Orange twist, garnish

Pour all ingredients, except gar-
nish, into a glass with ice.
Garnish with orange twist.
Makes 1 serving.

TENNESSEE TWISTER

4 ounces CRAN•RASPBERRY®
raspberry cranberry juice
drink
4 ounces unsweetened iced tea
1 ounce vodka
1/2 ounce pepper-flavored
vodka
2 teaspoons sugar

Combine all ingredients in a
glass, stirring to dissolve sugar.
Add ice. Makes 1 serving.

PEACHTREE PUNCH

6 ounces OCEAN SPRAY® Ruby
Red grapefruit juice drink
1 ounce vodka
3/4 ounce peach schnapps

Pour all ingredients into a glass
with ice. Makes 1 serving.

BEETLE JUICE

8 ounces CITRUS REFRESH-
ERS™ citrus peach juice
drink
1/2 ounce lemon-flavored vodka
1/2 ounce tropical schnapps
1/2 ounce blue curaçao
Peach wedge, garnish

Pour all ingredients, except gar-
nish, into a glass with ice.
Garnish with peach wedge.
Makes 1 serving.

MEXICAN MADRAS

3 ounces CRAN•RASPBERRY®
raspberry cranberry juice drink
1/2 ounce orange juice
1 ounce gold tequila
Dash lime juice
Orange slice, garnish

Pour all ingredients, except garnish, into a shaker half-filled with ice. Shake well. Strain into a glass. Garnish with orange slice. Makes 1 serving.

CRANBERRY MARGARITA

3 ounces CRAN•RASPBERRY®
raspberry cranberry juice drink
1 ounce gold tequila
Dash lime juice
Lime wedge, garnish

Pour all ingredients, except garnish, into a glass with ice. Garnish with lime wedge. Makes 1 serving.

TEQUILA LIME RICKEY

3 ounces CRAN•RASPBERRY®
raspberry cranberry juice drink
1 ounce gold tequila
Dash lime juice
Club soda
Lime wedge, garnish

Pour raspberry cranberry drink, tequila and lime juice into a glass with ice. Top with club soda. Garnish with lime wedge. Makes 1 serving.

IN THE MEXICAN MADRAS, CRANBERRY MARGARITA AND TEQUILA LIME RICKEY (CLOCKWISE FROM LEFT), CRANBERRIES MIX AND MATCH WITH MEXICAN SPIRITS.

ROADHOUSE REBEL

4 ounces OCEAN SPRAY®
  cranberry juice cocktail
4 ounces unsweetened iced tea
1 ounce vodka
1/2 ounce pepper vodka
2 teaspoons sugar

Combine all ingredients in a
glass, stirring to dissolve sugar.
Add ice. Makes 1 serving.

CRANBERRY BLAST

7 ounces CITRUS REFRESH-
  ERS™ citrus cranberry juice
  drink
1/2 ounce blackberry schnapps
1/2 ounce vodka
1/2 ounce triple sec

Pour all ingredients into a glass
with ice. Makes 1 serving.

WHOLE BERRY SAUCE LABEL, CIRCA 1923.

SOUTHERN SLAMMER

6 ounces CRAN•RASPBERRY®
  raspberry cranberry juice
  drink
1/2 ounce almond-flavored
  liqueur
1/2 ounce peach-flavored
  whiskey
1/2 ounce dry gin

Pour all ingredients into a glass
with ice. Makes 1 serving.

MANDARIN MIXER

5 ounces OCEAN SPRAY® Ruby
  Red & tangerine grapefruit
  juice drink
1 ounce vodka
1 ounce orange juice
Orange slice, garnish

Pour all ingredients, except
garnish, into a glass with ice.
Garnish with orange slice.
Makes 1 serving.

RUBY BEACH TEA

6 ounces OCEAN SPRAY®
  Ruby Red grapefruit
  juice drink
1/2 ounce vodka
1/2 ounce gin
1/2 ounce rum
1/2 ounce tequila

Pour all ingredients into a glass
with ice. Makes 1 serving.

SALTY BREEZE

3 ounces OCEAN SPRAY®
  cranberry juice cocktail
3 ounces OCEAN SPRAY® Ruby
  Red grapefruit juice drink
2 ounces vodka

Pour all ingredients into a glass
with ice. Makes 1 serving.

CRANBERRY VODKA

1 cup plain or citrus-flavored vodka
1 cup coarsely chopped OCEAN SPRAY® fresh or frozen cranberries

Combine ingredients in a small glass or plastic container. Cover and let sit at room temperature for 1 week.

Strain into a decorative glass decanter. Serve on the rocks or in mixed drinks. Makes 1 cup.

CRANBERRY KAKADU

7 ounces OCEAN SPRAY® cranberry juice cocktail
1 1/2 ounces coffee liqueur

Pour into a glass with ice. Makes 1 serving.

FESTIVE FRUIT PUNCH

1 48-ounce bottle CRAN•RASP-BERRY® raspberry cranberry juice drink, chilled
2 1/4 cups orange juice, chilled
1 cup pineapple juice, chilled
1 cup vodka, optional

Combine all ingredients in a large punch bowl. Garnish with an ice ring. Makes about 48 4-ounce servings.

FORTUNE TEA

8 ounces OCEAN SPRAY® Ruby Red grapefruit juice drink
1 1/4 ounces melon-flavored liqueur
Pineapple wedge, garnish

Pour all ingredients, except garnish, into a glass with ice. Garnish with pineapple wedge. Makes 1 serving.

GREAT WONDERS

4 ounces MAUNA LA'I® ¡MANGO-MANGO!™ mango Hawaiian guava juice drink
Dash grenadine
Club soda
Cherry, garnish

Pour juice drink and grenadine into a glass with ice. Top with club soda. Garnish with cherry. Makes 1 serving.

BILLABONG BERRY

8 ounces OCEAN SPRAY® cranberry juice cocktail
1 ounce blackberry brandy
1/2 ounce white brandy

Heat all ingredients in a saucepan or microwave. Serve in a mug. Makes 1 serving.

OCEAN SPRAY BRAND

"Pure fruit at less cost. Made from selected vine ripened cranberries which contain iron, iodine, lime, sugar and mild healthful acids. Packed in family and hotel sizes. American etiquette and patriotism demands it always be served with chicken, however used. Try in Salads, Decorations, Pies, Puddings."

CAPE COD CRANBERRY SAUCE
WHOLE FRUIT SWEETENED - READY TO SERVE

CHAPTER 3

NON-ALCOHOLIC DRINKS

RAZZLE DAZZLE LEMONADE

10 ounces CRAN•
RASPBERRY® raspberry
cranberry juice drink
6 ounces lemonade
Mint leaves, garnish

Pour ingredients, except garnish, into a 16-ounce glass with ice. Garnish with mint leaves. Makes 1 serving.

SLAM DUNK

4 ounces OCEAN SPRAY®
grapefruit juice
2 ounces orange juice
1 ounce cream of coconut
1/2 cup crushed ice
Orange slice, garnish

Put all ingredients, except garnish, in a blender. Blend on high speed for a few seconds or until ingredients are thoroughly combined. Pour into a glass. Garnish with orange slice. Makes 1 serving.

PRECEDING: RAZZLE DAZZLE LEMONADE. LEFT: STRAWBERRY BANANA SWIRL AND SLAM DUNK ARE QUICK AND EASY FROZEN BLENDER DRINKS.

CRANBERRY LEMONADE

8 ounces OCEAN SPRAY®
cranberry juice cocktail
4 ounces lemonade
Lemon slice, garnish

Pour ingredients, except garnish, into a large glass with ice. Garnish with lemon slice. Makes 1 serving.

STRAWBERRY BANANA SWIRL

FIRST SWIRL:
1/2 banana
3 ounces orange juice
1 cup crushed ice

SECOND SWIRL:
3 ounces CRAN•STRAW-
BERRY™ cranberry
strawberry juice drink
2 ounces thawed frozen
strawberries
3/4 ounce grenadine
1 cup crushed ice

Put all ingredients for first swirl in a blender. Blend on high speed for a few seconds or until ingredients are thoroughly combined. Pour into a pitcher; set aside.

Put all ingredients for second swirl in blender. Blend on high speed for a few seconds or until ingredients are thoroughly combined.

Simultaneously pour both mixtures into a large glass. Makes 1 serving.

WAKE-UP CALL

6 ounces CRAN•CHERRY™
cherry cranberry juice drink
2 ounces orange juice
1/2 banana

Put ingredients in a blender.
Blend for a few seconds on high
speed or until ingredients are
thoroughly combined. Makes 1
serving.

CHOCOLATE COVERED CHERRY

6 ounces CRAN•CHERRY™
cherry cranberry juice drink
2/3 cup chocolate ice cream
Cherry, garnish

Put ingredients, except garnish,
in a blender. Blend for a few
seconds on high speed or until
ingredients are thoroughly combined. Garnish with cherry.
Makes 1 serving.

SMOOTH SAILING

5 ounces OCEAN SPRAY® Ruby
Red grapefruit juice drink
2 ounces pineapple juice
2 ounces clear lemon-lime soda
Pineapple slice, garnish

Pour all ingredients, except gar-
nish, into a glass with ice.
Garnish with pineapple slice.
Makes 1 serving.

RUBY SOUR

5 ounces OCEAN SPRAY® Ruby
Red grapefruit juice drink
4 ounces lemonade
Lemon slice, garnish

Pour ingredients, except
garnish, into a glass with ice.
Garnish with lemon slice. Makes
1 serving.

CRANBERRY LIME RICKEY

8 ounces OCEAN SPRAY®
cranberry juice cocktail
2 teaspoons sugar
1 lime wedge
6 ounces clear lemon-lime soda
Lime wedge, garnish

Put cranberry juice cocktail and
sugar in a blender. Blend for a
few seconds on high speed until
the sugar is dissolved. Pour into
a large glass with ice. Squeeze
the lime wedge and add to glass.
Top with soda. Garnish with lime
wedge. Makes 1 serving.

PINKY

5 ounces OCEAN SPRAY® pink
grapefruit juice cocktail
2 ounces pineapple juice
1 ounce orange juice
1 tablespoon lime juice

Pour all ingredients into a glass
with ice. Makes 1 serving.

CATCH THE WAVE

6 ounces CRAN•CHERRY™
cherry cranberry juice drink
1 ounce pineapple juice
1/2 ounce cream of coconut

Put all ingredients in a blender.
Blend for a few seconds on high
speed. Makes 1 serving.

CRANBERRY ICED TEA

4 ounces OCEAN SPRAY®
cranberry juice cocktail
4 ounces unsweetened tea
2 teaspoons sugar
Lemon wedge, garnish

Put cranberry juice cocktail and
tea in a glass. Add sugar; stir
until completely dissolved. Add
ice. Garnish with lemon wedge.
Makes 1 serving.

PUCKER PUSS

5 ounces OCEAN SPRAY®
grapefruit juice
3 ounces CRAN•RASPBERRY®
raspberry cranberry juice
drink
Club soda

Pour grapefruit juice and
raspberry cranberry drink
into a glass with ice. Top with
club soda; stir gently. Makes
1 serving.

BEACHCOMBER

5 ounces OCEAN SPRAY®
   grapefruit juice
3 ounces OCEAN SPRAY®
   cranberry juice cocktail
Club soda

Pour grapefruit juice and cranberry juice cocktail into a glass with ice. Top with club soda; stir gently. Makes 1 serving.

TRADE WINDS

8 ounces OCEAN SPRAY® pink
   grapefruit juice cocktail
1/4 cup frozen vanilla yogurt
1/2 teaspoon cream of coconut

Put all ingredients in a blender. Blend for a few seconds on high speed or until ingredients are thoroughly combined. Pour into a glass. Makes 1 serving.

CRANBERRY KISS

6 ounces OCEAN SPRAY®
   cranberry juice cocktail
1 ounce orange juice
Club soda

Pour cranberry juice cocktail and orange juice into a glass with ice. Top with club soda. Makes 1 serving.

RUBY COOLER

8 ounces OCEAN SPRAY® Ruby
   Red grapefruit juice drink
1 ounce cream of coconut
1/2 cup vanilla ice cream

Put all ingredients in a blender. Blend for a few seconds on high speed or until ingredients are thoroughly combined. Makes 1 serving.

AN EARLY CRANBERRY JUICE COCKTAIL BOTTLE, CIRCA 1944.

SLING SHOT

6 ounces OCEAN SPRAY® pink
   grapefruit juice cocktail
1/4 cup frozen raspberries
1/4 cup frozen vanilla yogurt

Put all ingredients in a blender. Blend for a few seconds on high speed or until ingredients are thoroughly combined. Pour into a glass. Makes 1 serving.

SANGRIA PARTY PUNCH

1 48-ounce bottle CITRUS
   REFRESHERS™ citrus
   cranberry juice drink, chilled
2 1/2 cups pineapple orange
   juice, chilled
2 1/2 cups sparkling Concord
   grape juice, chilled
2 1/2 cups seltzer water, chilled
Orange, lemon and lime slices,
   garnish

Combine all ingredients, except garnishes, in a medium punch bowl. Garnish with orange, lemon and lime slices. Makes about 24 4-ounce servings.

PERFECT PARTY PUNCH

2 64-ounce bottles OCEAN
   SPRAY® Ruby Red grapefruit
   juice drink, chilled
1/2 cup thawed limeade
   concentrate
1 cup raspberry-lime seltzer
   water, chilled
1 pint raspberry or lime
   sherbet, softened

Combine all ingredients, except sherbet, in a large punch bowl. Float softened sherbet on top of punch just before serving. Makes about 32 4-ounce servings.

CRANBERRY WASSAIL

1 gallon OCEAN SPRAY® cranberry juice cocktail
5 cups apple juice
2/3 cup sugar
4 3-inch cinnamon sticks
2 teaspoons whole allspice
1 medium orange, sliced
20 whole cloves
2 1/2 cups brandy or vodka, optional
Orange slices, garnish
Whole cloves, garnish

Combine cranberry juice cocktail, apple juice, sugar, cinnamon sticks and allspice in a large pot. Heat to boiling over medium heat; reduce heat and simmer 10 minutes. Strain punch to remove spices. Serve warm in a heat proof punch bowl or chill and serve over ice. For a more spirited punch, stir brandy into hot punch or vodka into chilled punch. Garnish with orange slices studded with cloves. Makes 42 4-ounce servings.

PINK SENSATION

6 ounces OCEAN SPRAY® pink grapefruit juice cocktail
1/2 cup raspberry sorbet

Put ingredients in a blender. Blend for a few seconds on high speed or until ingredients are thoroughly combined. Pour into a glass. Makes 1 serving.

PARADISE FOUND

5 ounces OCEAN SPRAY® pink grapefruit juice cocktail
2 ounces pineapple juice
Lemon-lime soda
Orange slice, garnish

Pour grapefruit juice cocktail and pineapple juice into a glass with ice. Top with soda. Garnish with orange slice. Makes 1 serving.

SWEET DREAMS

5 ounces MAUNA LA'I® ISLAND GUAVA™ Hawaiian guava juice drink
2 ounces lemon-lime soda
1 ounce pineapple juice
1 teaspoon lime juice
Pineapple slice, garnish

Pour all ingredients, except garnish, into a glass with ice. Garnish with pineapple slice. Makes 1 serving.

SWEET DREAMS OFFERS A MEDLEY OF TROPICAL FLAVORS.

Cherry Cookie Crunch Punch

1 48-ounce bottle CRAN•CHERRY™ cherry cranberry juice drink
1 cup vanilla syrup
1 quart cookies-and-cream ice cream
2 cups raspberry ginger ale
Whipped cream, garnish
Crushed chocolate sandwich cookies, garnish
Maraschino cherries, garnish

Combine cherry cranberry drink, vanilla syrup and ice cream in a large punch bowl. Use a rotary beater or wire whisk to thoroughly combine ingredients until creamy. Gently stir in raspberry ginger ale just before serving. Garnish with whipped cream. Sprinkle with crushed cookies and top with cherries. Makes about 32 4-ounce servings.

Raspberry Iced Tea

4 ounces CRAN•RASPBERRY® raspberry cranberry juice drink
4 ounces unsweetened tea
1 teaspoon sugar
Mint leaves, garnish

Pour raspberry cranberry drink and tea in a glass. Add sugar; stir until completely dissolved. Add ice and garnish. Makes 1 serving.

Luscious Strawberry Party Punch

1 48-ounce bottle CRAN•STRAWBERRY™ cranberry strawberry juice drink, chilled
2 quarts strawberry ice milk or ice cream, softened
2 cups frozen strawberries, thawed
2 12-ounce cans lemon-lime soda, chilled

Combined cranberry strawberry drink, ice milk and strawberries in a large punch bowl. Use a rotary beater or wire whisk to thoroughly combine ingredients until creamy. Gently stir in soda just before serving. Makes about 50 1/3-cup servings.

Fountain of Youth

5 ounces MAUNA LA'I® ISLAND GUAVA™ Hawaiian guava juice drink
1 ounce pineapple juice
2 whole strawberries
1/2 cup vanilla ice cream or vanilla frozen yogurt
Strawberry, garnish

Put all ingredients, except garnish in a blender. Blend for a few seconds on high speed or until ingredients are thoroughly combined. Garnish with strawberry. Makes 1 serving.

Blushed Berry

6 ounces OCEAN SPRAY® cranberry juice cocktail
5 ounces MAUNA LA'I® ISLAND GUAVA™ Hawaiian guava juice drink
6 ounces tonic water

Mix cranberry juice cocktail and guava fruit drink in a small pitcher. Stir in tonic water. Serve over ice. Makes 2 servings.

Frosty Citrus Freeze

6 ounces OCEAN SPRAY® grapefruit juice
1/2 cup fruit flavored frozen yogurt

Put all ingredients in a blender. Blend for a few seconds on high speed or until ingredients are thoroughly combined. Pour into a glass. Makes 1 serving.

Kawaihini

12 ounces MAUNA LA'I® PARADISE PASSION™ Hawaiian guava passion juice drink
1 cup chocolate ice cream, softened slightly

Put all ingredients in a blender. Blend for a few seconds on high speed or until ingredients are thoroughly combined. Makes 2 servings.

BELOW: *A GLASS BOTTLE LABEL FROM 1945. LEFT: PREWAR LABEL.*

CREAMY CITRUS COOLER

4 ounces OCEAN SPRAY® pink grapefruit juice cocktail or OCEAN SPRAY® grapefruit juice
4 ounces orange juice
4 ounces pineapple juice
1/2 cup low-fat vanilla ice cream

Put all ingredients in a blender. Blend for a few seconds on high speed or until ingredients are thoroughly combined. Makes 2 servings.

CREAMY CRANBERRY COOLER

2 ounces CRAN•RASPBERRY® raspberry cranberry juice drink
2 ounces orange juice
2 ounces pineapple juice
2 ounces cream
1/4 ounce grenadine
4 ounces crushed ice

Put all ingredients in a blender. Blend on high speed for a few seconds or until ingredients are thoroughly combined. Makes 1 serving.

RASPBERRY KISS

6 ounces CRAN•RASPBERRY® raspberry cranberry juice drink
1 ounce orange juice
1/4 teaspoon lime juice
Club soda

Pour raspberry cranberry drink, orange juice and lime juice into a tall glass with ice. Top with club soda. Makes 1 serving.

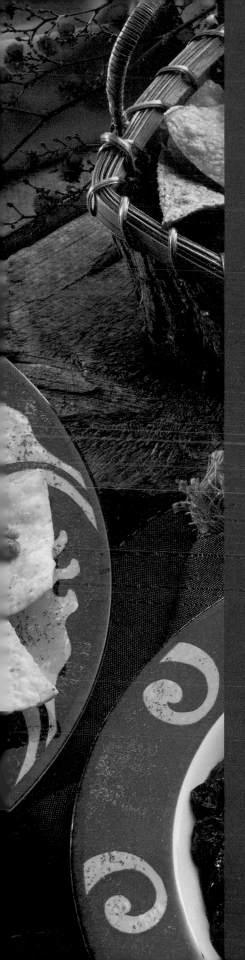

CHAPTER 4

DAZZLING APPETIZERS

SOUTHWESTERN CHICKEN NACHOS

· · · · · · · · · · · · · · · ·

1 12-ounce package
   CRAN•FRUIT™ cranberry
   raspberry crushed fruit
1 green onion, white and green
   parts, sliced
3 tablespoons chopped canned
   jalapeño peppers
2 tablespoons lime juice
1 1/2 teaspoons cumin
1 teaspoon dried cilantro
1 pound ground chicken
1 1 1/4-ounce envelope taco
   seasoning mix
1/2 cup water
6 ounces nacho chips
1 cup shredded Monterey
   Jack cheese

Combine crushed fruit, green onion, jalapeños, lime juice, cumin and cilantro in a medium mixing bowl. Set aside.

Place chicken in a large non-stick frying pan. Cook on medium heat until no longer pink. Break meat into small pieces during cooking. Drain excess liquid. Add taco seasoning and water. Simmer on medium heat for about 5 minutes or until liquid is absorbed, stirring frequently.

Place nacho chips on a jelly roll pan. Spoon chicken over chips. Top with crushed fruit mixture and cheese. Broil until cheese melts and begins to bubble. Makes 6–8 servings.

CRANBERRY SHRIMP COCKTAIL SAUCE

· · · · · · · · · · · · · · · · · · ·

2 1/4 cups OCEAN SPRAY®
   fresh or frozen cranberries
1/2 cup water
1/2 cup sugar
1 cup brown sugar
1/2 cup chili sauce
1/4 cup and 2 tablespoons
   vinegar
1/4 cup chopped onion
1/4 cup Worcestershire sauce

Bring cranberries, water and sugar to a boil in a medium saucepan. Cook until the berries pop. Place a wire mesh strainer over a medium mixing bowl. Pour contents of saucepan into strainer. Press cranberries with the back of a spoon, frequently scraping the outside of the strainer, until no pulp is left. Stir contents of bowl.

Combine remaining ingredients with puree in a medium saucepan. Bring to a boil. Reduce heat and simmer until sauce thickens, about 20 minutes. Stir sauce frequently. Cool to room temperature before serving. Makes about 2 cups.

PRECEDING: SOUTHWESTERN CHICKEN NACHOS. LEFT: ONCE THE LARGEST INDEPENDENT DISTRIBUTOR IN MASSACHUSETTS, THE BEATON FAMILY GREW, PACKAGED AND SOLD CRANBERRIES UNDER THEIR OWN NAME.

CRANBERRY TURKEY WONTONS

1 16-ounce can OCEAN SPRAY® whole berry cranberry sauce
1 1/2 cups cooked turkey, finely chopped
1 cup onion, finely diced
1 1/2 tablespoons soy sauce
1 16-ounce package wonton wrappers
2 tablespoons margarine or butter, melted

Preheat oven to 375 degrees. Grease a jelly roll pan.

Combine cranberry sauce, turkey, onion and soy sauce in a large mixing bowl. Spoon 1 rounded teaspoon of filling in the center of a wonton wrapper. Lightly brush edges with water. Bring two opposite corners together over filling, pinching edges together to seal. Repeat on opposite side. Continue until all of the filling is used. Wrap up any remaining wonton wrappers for another use. Place wontons on prepared pan.

Brush wontons with margarine. Bake for 10 minutes or until crisp and golden brown. Makes about 20 wontons.

CRANBERRY CHICKEN SATAY

3 bamboo skewers
1/4 cup CRAN•FRUIT™ crushed fruit
2 tablespoons peanut butter
2 teaspoons soy sauce
2 teaspoons lemon juice
4 garlic cloves, finely minced
1 teaspoon crushed red pepper
1 pound chicken tenders

Soak skewers in a bowl of water for 30 minutes.

Mix all ingredients, except chicken, in a food processor or blender. Process for 30 seconds or until the mixture is well mixed with small chunks.

Thread meat on skewers. Brush with half of the crushed fruit mixture. Grill or broil until chicken is no longer pink. Turn skewers and brush with sauce frequently during cooking. Use remaining crushed fruit mixture for dipping. Makes 3 servings.

Use as a jelly

Crush the sauce with a fork for pie filling. Bake with crust or just fill and frost.

CRANBERRY BRUSCHETTA

1 1/2 cups OCEAN SPRAY® fresh or frozen cranberries
1/4 cup sugar
2 tablespoons red wine vinegar
1/2 red onion, thinly sliced into rings
2 garlic cloves, minced
2 tablespoons minced fresh basil
1 teaspoon oregano
Oil
1 8-ounce loaf French bread

Combine cranberries, sugar and red wine vinegar in a medium saucepan. Bring to a boil. Add onion and garlic, return to a boil and reduce heat. Simmer on low for 10 minutes or until cranberries pop.

Pour into a glass bowl. Stir in basil and oregano. Cool at room temperature.

Cut bread diagonally into 16 3/4-inch slices; brush both sides with oil. Broil each side for 1 to 2 minutes or until golden brown. Top each slice with cranberry mixture. Makes 16 servings.

DIFFERENT USES FOR CRANBERRY SAUCE WERE PROMOTED AS EARLY AS THE 1920s.

BRIE AND CRANBERRY PHYLLO TRIANGLES

1 pound phyllo dough
3/4-1 cup melted butter
1 16-ounce can OCEAN SPRAY® whole berry
   cranberry sauce
1/2 pound Brie cheese, cut into 1/2-inch cubes

Preheat oven to 350 degrees. Cut phyllo dough in half lengthwise. Keep covered with plastic wrap while working.

Place 2 sheets of phyllo dough on work surface; brush with butter. Fold in half lengthwise; brush with butter.

Place 1 1/2 teaspoons of cranberry sauce and 6 cubes of Brie at bottom of strip. Fold corner over filling. Fold up, then over the opposite way, forming a triangle. Continue folding this way until the end. Brush with butter and place on a jelly roll pan. Repeat with remaining phyllo dough and filling.

Bake for 10 minutes or until golden brown. Cool 5 minutes before serving. Makes 20–25 appetizers.

CRANBERRY TURKEY WALDORF SALAD

BATTER:
1/2 cup flour
2 tablespoons sugar
1/2 cup milk
1 egg

SALAD:
2 cups cooked turkey, cut into 1/2-inch pieces
1 cup apple, peeled and cut into 1/2-inch pieces
1/2 cup celery, diced
1/4 cup chopped walnuts
1 cup OCEAN SPRAY® whole berry cranberry sauce
1/4 cup mayonnaise
Red leaf lettuce, garnish

Preheat oven to 400 degrees. Grease a 9-inch pie plate.

Combine all batter ingredients in a medium mixing bowl. Beat using an electric mixer for 1 minute. Pour batter into prepared pan. Bake for 20 minutes or until golden brown. If center has puffed, place a clean potholder or dish towel on top and gently press down. Set aside.

Combine turkey, apple, celery and walnuts in a large mixing bowl. Combine cranberry sauce and mayonnaise in a separate bowl. Add to turkey mixture, mixing well.

Line pancake with lettuce. Place salad inside. Chill until serving time. Makes 6–8 servings.

ORIENTAL CHICKEN SALAD

5 ounces dried Chinese noodles
3 tablespoons olive oil
2 tablespoons frozen orange juice
  concentrate, thawed
1 teaspoon coarsely ground pepper
3/4 teaspoon garlic powder
1/4 teaspoon ginger
1 6-ounce package CRAISINS® sweetened
  dried cranberries
1 11-ounce can Mandarin oranges, drained
3 green onions, white and green parts, sliced
1 pound chicken tenders
2-3 tablespoons poppy seeds
2 tablespoons oil

Cook noodles (without flavor packet, if included) according to package directions. Rinse with cold water; drain thoroughly. Set aside.

Combine olive oil, orange juice concentrate, pepper, garlic powder and ginger, mixing vigorously with a fork. Add to noodles, tossing to mix. Gently toss in dried cranberries, oranges and green onions. Place in serving bowl; set aside.

Rinse chicken with cool water; pat dry. Sprinkle poppy seeds on a plate. Press one side of each chicken tender into poppy seeds.

Heat oil in a medium frying pan. Place chicken, poppy seed side down, in the pan. Cook until chicken is no longer pink inside, about 5 minutes, turning only once. Place chicken on top of noodles. Makes 3 servings.

FRUITED BRIE BAKE

1 15-ounce wheel Brie cheese
1/2 cup OCEAN SPRAY® whole berry
  cranberry sauce
1/2 cup apricot preserves
Sliced almonds

Preheat oven to 350 degrees.

Slice off the top 1/4 inch of the Brie wheel; set aside. Hollow out the center of the cheese, leaving a 1-inch shell all around. Place in an ovenproof serving container slightly larger than cheese. Save leftover cheese for another use.

Break up cranberry sauce with a fork and place in center of cheese. Cover with top of cheese. Spoon apricot preserves over top; sprinkle with almonds.

Bake for 8–10 minutes or until soft and slightly melted. Serve with crackers. Makes 8 servings.

OPPOSITE: QUICK, EASY AND ELEGANT, FRUITED BRIE BAKE MAKES A SMASHING APPETIZER.

SMOKED TURKEY APPETIZERS

1 pound phyllo dough
3/4-1 cup melted butter
1 1/4 cups OCEAN SPRAY® whole berry
    cranberry sauce
1/4 pound smoked deli turkey, coarsely chopped

Preheat oven to 350 degrees. Cut phyllo dough in half lengthwise. Keep covered with plastic wrap while working.

Place 2 sheets of dough on work surface; brush with butter. Fold in half lengthwise; brush with butter. Place 1 1/2 teaspoons of cranberry sauce and 1 teaspoon of smoked turkey at the bottom of strip. Fold corner over filling. Fold up, then over the opposite way, forming a triangle. Continue folding this way until the end. Brush triangle with butter; place on a jelly roll pan. Repeat with remaining phyllo dough and filing.

Bake for 10 minutes or until golden brown. Cool about 5 minutes before serving. Makes 20-25 appetizers.

BOURSIN AND BACON APPETIZERS

1 17 1/4-ounce package frozen
    puff pastry dough
3/4 cup CRAN•FRUIT™ cranberry raspberry
    crushed fruit
1 4-ounce package Boursin cheese, softened
11 bacon strips, cooked and crumbled

Defrost pastry as directed on package. Preheat oven to 375 degrees.

Cut each pastry sheet into sixteen 2 1/2 x 2 1/2-inch squares. Press each pastry square into a mini-muffin tin. Place 1 rounded measuring teaspoon of crushed fruit in each pastry shell. Top with 1/2 rounded measuring teaspoon of cheese. Sprinkle with bacon bits.

Bake for 20 minutes or until pastry shells are golden brown. Makes 32 appetizers.

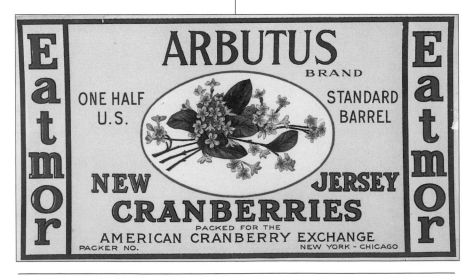

ABOVE: ARBUTUS WAS ONE OF NEARLY 45 BRANDS UNDER NEW ENGLAND GROWERS' EATMOR CLASSIFICATIONS. OPPOSITE: CRANBERRY SAUCE ADVERTISEMENT, CIRCA 1920.

Ocean Spray
BRAND

TO
SERVE

CAPE COD
CRANBERRY SAUCE
STRAINED AND SWEETENED

Individual Ser

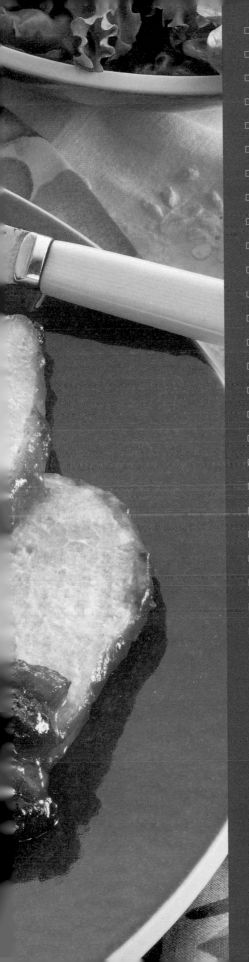

CHAPTER 5

GLAZES, MARINADES, & SAUCES

AMERICAN BEAUTY BRAND

NEW JERSEY CRANBERRIES

PACKED BY
GROWERS CRANBERRY CO.

Packer No.

FOR
AMERICAN CRANBERRY EXCHANGE
NEW YORK, CHICAGO, U.S.A.

QUICKIE CRANBERRY GRILLING SAUCES

SAUCE BASE:
1 16-ounce can OCEAN SPRAY® jellied cranberry sauce
1 10-ounce jar apricot preserves
1/4 cup vinegar
2 tablespoons Worcestershire sauce

HOT SEASONING:
1/4 teaspoon cayenne pepper
1 tablespoon diced canned hot jalepeño peppers
3 tablespoons finely chopped sweet onion

Combine base ingredients with your choice of ONE hot seasoning, in a medium saucepan. Bring to a boil over high heat. Whisk vigorously and frequently. Reduce heat to a low boil. Simmer 10 minutes, whisking occasionally.

Cool to room temperature or chill until needed. Use as a grilling sauce for poultry, pork or beef. Makes about 2 cups.

PRECEDING: CRANBERRY CHUTNEY (PAGE 56), CRANBERRY MAPLE GLAZE (PAGE 57). RIGHT: EVEN THOUGH NO LONGER USED, THE BARREL IS STILL THE STANDARD UNIT OF MEASURE FOR CRANBERRIES.

FRUIT JUICE JELLIES

2 cups OCEAN SPRAY® Ruby Red grapefruit juice cocktail or CRANAPPLE® cranberry apple juice drink
2 cups sugar
1 envelope liquid pectin

Combine juice drink and sugar in a medium saucepan. Bring to a FULL rolling boil over high heat, stirring frequently. Add pectin and return mixture to a FULL rolling boil for 1 minute, stirring frequently. Remove mixture from heat and skim off foam.

Pour jellies into sterilized jars and seal with melted paraffin wax. Let cool until the jars have reached room temperature and then place in refrigerator until set. Makes 2 1/2 pints.

SANTE FE CRANBERRY RELISH

1 12-ounce package OCEAN SPRAY® fresh or frozen cranberries
3/4 cup sugar
1 medium jalepeño, cut into quarters
1 green onion, cut into quarters
1 teaspoon dried cilantro
Scant 1/4 teaspoon cumin

Put all ingredients in a food processor. Process until the mixture is coarsely chopped. Store in refrigerator overnight to allow flavors to blend. Makes about 3 cups.

CRANBERRY VINAIGRETTE DRESSING

1 cup OCEAN SPRAY® jellied cranberry sauce
2 tablespoons vinegar
1 tablespoon sugar
1/8 teaspoon cardamom
1/2 cup oil

Blend cranberry sauce, vinegar, sugar and cardamom for a few seconds in blender. With blender running, SLOWLY add oil through the hole in the lid. Makes 1 cup.

CAPE COD BBQ SAUCE

1 16-ounce can OCEAN SPRAY®
  jellied cranberry sauce
1/2 cup chili sauce
1/2 cup brown sugar
1/4 cup finely chopped sweet
  onion
1/4 cup vinegar
1/4 cup Worcestershire sauce

Combine all ingredients in a medium saucepan. Bring to a boil over high heat. Whisk vigorously and frequently. Reduce heat to a low boil. Simmer 20 minutes, whisking occasionally.

Cool to room temperature or chill until needed. Use as a barbecue sauce for poultry, pork or beef. Makes 2 cups.

BERRY CHILI BARBECUE SAUCE

1 16-ounce can OCEAN SPRAY®
  jellied cranberry sauce
3/4 cup chili sauce
2 tablespoons Worcestershire
  sauce
1 tablespoon lemon juice

Combine all ingredients in a medium saucepan. Cook over medium heat, stirring occasionally, until the cranberry sauce has melted. Use as a baste for broiling or grilling meat or poultry; also good as a dipping sauce. Makes about 2 1/2 cups.

CRANBERRY SWEET AND SOUR SAUCE

1/4 cup brown sugar
1 tablespoon cornstarch
3/4 cup OCEAN SPRAY® whole
  berry cranberry sauce
3/4 cup pineapple juice
1/4 cup cider vinegar
1 1/2 tablespoons soy sauce

Combine brown sugar and cornstarch in a medium saucepan. Add cranberry sauce, pineapple juice, vinegar and soy sauce. Cook over medium heat, stirring constantly, until thickened. Serve as a sauce for chicken or pork. Makes about 2 cups.

CRANBERRY VINEGAR

1 cup vinegar
1 cup OCEAN SPRAY® fresh or
  frozen cranberries

Combine ingredients in a small saucepan. Bring to a boil. Reduce heat and boil gently until the cranberries pop. Pour into a glass or plastic container. Cover and let sit at room temperature for 3 days.

Strain vinegar into a decorative glass bottle. (Strain through a cheesecloth-lined strainer for a clearer vinegar.) Makes 1 cup.

CURRIED CITRUS MARINADE

1 cup OCEAN SPRAY®
  grapefruit juice
2 tablespoons olive oil
2 tablespoons soy sauce
1 teaspoon sugar
1 teaspoon curry powder
1/2 teaspoon salt
1/2 teaspoon white pepper
4 boneless, skinless chicken
  breast halves

Combine all ingredients, except chicken, in a non-metal bowl or resealable plastic bag. Poke both sides of chicken with a fork. Put chicken in marinade; cover bowl or reseal bag. Refrigerate overnight, turning chicken occasionally. Bake or grill chicken, basting with marinade, if desired. Makes 1 cup.

CRANBERRY HONEY GLAZE

1 8-ounce can OCEAN SPRAY®
  jellied cranberry sauce
1/4 cup honey

Combine ingredients in a small saucepan. Cook over medium heat just until sauce is smooth, whisking frequently.

Liberally brush on poultry or ham during cooking. Makes about 1 cup.

AND PUNCH HOLE IN OPPOSITE END TO LET IN AIR.
CONTENTS WILL SLIDE OUT AS SOLID JELLY

MADE FROM
CRANBERRIES
WATER
SUGAR
CORN SYRUP
NET WT. 1 LB.

Serves 8

Packed by
NATIONAL CRANBERRY
ASSOCIATION
HEADQUARTERS
HANSON, MASS.
Branches
ONSET, MASS.
NORTH CHICAGO, ILL.
BORDENTOWN, N. J.
MARKHAM, WASH.
COQUILLE, ORE.
COPYRIGHT 1947
NATIONAL CRANBERRY ASSOC.
PRINTED IN U.S.A.

Ocean Spray

Serve with
Chicken or Turkey

Ready to Serve

Guaranteed by
Good Housekeeping
REPLACEMENT OR A REFUND OF MONEY IF NOT AS ADVERTISED THEREIN

COMMENDED by PARENTS' MAGAZINE

Jellied
CRANBERRY SAUCE

IN THE EARLY 1950S, OCEAN SPRAY ENCOURAGED CRANBERRY SAUCE USAGE WITH POULTRY YEAR-ROUND.

CRANBERRY CHUTNEY

1 16-ounce can OCEAN SPRAY® whole berry
   cranberry sauce
1/2 cup raisins
1/2 cup peeled, diced apple
1/4 cup + 2 tablespoons sugar
1/4 cup + 2 tablespoons vinegar
1/8 teaspoon allspice
1/8 teaspoon ginger
1/8 teaspoon cinnamon
Dash ground cloves

Combine all ingredients in a medium saucepan.
Cook on medium heat, stirring occasionally, until
apples are tender and sauce has thickened slightly, about 30 minutes. Makes about 2 1/2 cups.

CRANBERRY JAM

4 1/2 cups OCEAN SPRAY® fresh or frozen
   cranberries
4 cups sugar
1 envelope liquid pectin

Sterilize jars and lids.

   Combine cranberries and sugar in a 6-quart
saucepan. Bring to a FULL, rolling boil over high
heat, stirring occasionally. Stir in pectin. Return to a
FULL rolling boil. Boil for 1 minute, stirring constantly. Remove from heat and skim off any foam.

   Fill jars. Wipe jar rims and cover with lids.
Invert for 5 minutes, then turn upright. Let cool
completely at room temperature. Check lids for
proper seal. Makes 2 pints.

CRANBERRY MAPLE GLAZE

1 8-ounce can OCEAN SPRAY® jellied cranberry sauce
1/4 cup maple syrup

Combine ingredients in a small saucepan. Cook over medium heat just until sauce is smooth, whisking frequently. Liberally brush on poultry or ham during cooking. Makes about 1 cup.

CRANBERRY MUSTARD SAUCE

1 16-ounce can OCEAN SPRAY® jellied cranberry sauce
2 tablespoons grainy mustard
1 1/2 tablespoon brown sugar

Combine all ingredients in a medium saucepan. Cook on medium heat until sauce is smooth, whisking occasionally. Serve over meat, poultry or shrimp. Makes 1 3/4 cups.

SWEET AND SOUR SALSA

1 cup OCEAN SPRAY® fresh or frozen cranberries
1/4 cup chopped red onion
1/2 cup chopped green pepper
1/4 cup sugar
1 teaspoon ginger
1/4 cup oil
1/2 cup pineapple chunks, cut in half
1 small tomato, chopped

Combine cranberries, onion, pepper, sugar, and ginger in a medium bowl. Heat oil in a skillet. Saute cranberry mixture just until cranberries begin to pop, stirring frequently.

Stir in pineapple and tomato. Cook until heated through.

Drain off any excess liquid. Transfer to serving bowl. Serve warm. Makes about 2 cups.

CRANBERRY APPLE FRUIT BUTTER

1 12-ounce package OCEAN SPRAY® fresh or frozen cranberries
1 cup OCEAN SPRAY® cranberry juice cocktail
3 cups peeled, diced apple
1 cup brown sugar
1 teaspoon cinnamon
1/2 teaspoon ginger
1/2 teaspoon nutmeg

Combine cranberries and cranberry juice cocktail in a medium saucepan. Bring mixture to a boil over medium heat. Cook just until the cranberries begin to pop, stirring frequently. Add remaining ingredients. Reduce heat and simmer, uncovered, for 1 1/2 hours, stirring occasionally.

Place a wire mesh strainer over a medium non-metal bowl. Pour contents of saucepan into strainer. Press with the back of a spoon, frequently scraping the outside of the strainer until no pulp is left. Place a piece of plastic directly over sauce. Cool to room temperature. Transfer to a non-metal storage container. Store covered in refrigerator for up to 2 weeks. Makes about 1 1/2 cups.

CHAPTER 6

Fast & Easy Recipes

TURKEY SALAD WITH CRANBERRY FETA CHEESE DRESSING

1 head red leaf lettuce
12-16 slices cooked turkey
1/2 cup coarsely chopped pecans
1 cup OCEAN SPRAY® whole berry
   cranberry sauce
2 tablespoons vinegar
1 tablespoon sugar
1 cup crumbled feta cheese
1/2 cup oil

Line 4 salad plates with lettuce. Arrange 3 or 4 slices of turkey on plates. Sprinkle each with 2 tablespoons of pecans. Set aside.

Put cranberry sauce, vinegar, sugar and half of the feta cheese in a blender. Blend for a few seconds on high speed. Remove the cap in the center of the blender lid; place lid back on blender. With the blender running, SLOWLY add oil through the hole in the lid. Stir in remaining feta cheese.

Serve salad with dressing drizzled on top or on the side in individual ramekins. Makes 4 salads.

SOUTH OF THE BORDER SAUCE

1/2 cup CRAN•FRUIT™ crushed fruit, cranberry
   raspberry or cranberry strawberry
1/2 cup corn syrup
1/2 cup hot sliced cherry peppers with liquid

Combine crushed fruit and corn syrup in a small saucepan. Chop peppers with liquid in a food processor; add to saucepan. Simmer 5 minutes. Serve over chicken. Makes about 1 cup.

CRANBERRY BOURSIN TURKEY CROISSANT

Spread softened Boursin cheese and CRAN•FRUIT™ crushed fruit on top half of a croissant. Place some red leaf lettuce and turkey slices on the bottom half. Place halves together.

Serve with a fresh garden salad and delicious cranberry vinaigrette salad dressing (see page 54).

PRECEDING: TURKEY SALAD WITH CRANBERRY FETA CHEESE DRESSING. ABOVE: IN 1946, THE CRANBERRY CANNERS, INC. CHANGED THEIR NAME TO THE NATIONAL CRANBERRY ASSOCIATION— LATER TO BECOME OCEAN SPRAY CRANBERRIES, INC. (LABEL, CIRCA 1946-53)

CORNBREAD CHICKEN PIE

1 11.5-ounce package refrigerated cornbread twists
2 cups cooked chicken, diced
1 cup CRAN•FRUIT™ crushed fruit, cranberry raspberry or cranberry strawberry
2 cups prepared stuffing
1 7-ounce package refrigerated cornbread twists

Preheat oven to 350 degrees.

To make the bottom crust, unroll the large tube of cornbread twists. Flatten with fingers and fit into bottom and sides of a 9-inch pie plate.

Place chicken in pie plate; top with crushed fruit. Add stuffing next. Unroll small tube of cornbread twists. Flatten with fingers and fit on top of pie to make the top crust.

Bake for 15 minutes. Cover with aluminum foil and bake 15 more minutes. Let sit 5 minutes before serving. Makes 4–6 servings.

TURKEY BURGERS

1 16-ounce can OCEAN SPRAY® jellied cranberry sauce
1 pound ground turkey
1/4 cup chopped onion
2 teaspoons coarsely ground black pepper
2 teaspoons dried parsley
4 hamburger buns

Put cranberry sauce in a medium mixing bowl; mash with a fork until smooth.

Thoroughly combine 1/3 cup of the cranberry sauce, ground turkey, onion, pepper and parsley. Divide mixture into 4 portions and shape into patties.

Place patties in a large skillet. Cook on medium heat until almost cooked, about 7 minutes. Flip burgers and cook to desired doneness.

Generously spread tops and bottoms of hamburger buns with remaining cranberry sauce. Place finished burgers on buns. Serve immediately. Makes 4 servings.

MECHANICAL PICKERS REPLACED HAND SCOOPS IN THE 1950S.

CRANBERRY RASPBERRY FONDUE

....

1 tablespoon cornstarch
1/4 cup water
1 16-ounce can OCEAN SPRAY® jellied
   cranberry sauce
   1/2 cup raspberry liqueur

Combine cornstarch and water in a small bowl. Set aside.

Melt cranberry sauce in a medium saucepan, whisking frequently. Add liqueur to saucepan. When mixture begins to boil, add the cornstarch mixture, whisking until sauce thickens.

Transfer to a fondue pot and keep warm with a low flame. Makes 2 cups. Savory dippers: cocktail meatballs, chicken nuggets, sausage pieces. Sweet dippers: pirouette cookies, coconut macaroons, meringues, pound cake, fruit.

CRANBERRY APPLE SCAMPI WITH SWEET PEPPERS

....

2 tablespoons butter or margarine
2 tablespoons shallots, finely diced
1 1/3 pounds frozen shrimp, defrosted
1/4 cup white wine
3 tablespoons red sweet pepper, diced
1 tablespoon curry powder
1 1/2 teaspoons almond extract
1 1/2 cups CRANAPPLE® cranberry apple juice
   drink
4 teaspoons fresh parsley, chopped
1/4 teaspoon salt
1/4 cup sliced almonds, toasted

Melt butter or margarine over medium heat in a large skillet. Add shallots and cook until tender and transparent. Add shrimp, stirring to coat with butter. Increase heat to medium high; add wine and 2 tablespoons red pepper. Cook until liquid is reduced by half.

Add curry, almond extract, cranberry apple drink, 2 teaspoons parsley and salt. Stir and continue cooking until liquid has thickened slightly. Transfer to serving dish. Garnish with toasted almonds and remaining red pepper and parsley. Serve over rice or pasta. Makes 4–6 servings.

LEFT: CRANBERRY RASPBERRY FONDUE COMPLEMENTS BOTH SWEET AND SAVORY DIPPERS.

BOURSIN BAKED CHICKEN

4 boneless chicken breast halves
1/2 cup milk
2 cups plain bread crumbs
1/4 cup butter or margarine, melted
2 4-ounce packages Boursin cheese, softened
Fresh parsley, minced
1 12-ounce package CRAN•FRUIT™ crushed fruit

Preheat oven to 350 degrees.

Dip each breast in milk and then into bread crumbs, coating both sides. Place chicken in a baking pan. Drizzle melted butter or margarine over chicken. Bake for 30 minutes or until chicken is no longer pink inside.

Remove chicken from oven. Carefully spread 1/4 cup Boursin cheese on each breast. Sprinkle with parsley. Return pan to oven and bake just until cheese begins to melt, about 2 minutes. Serve with crushed fruit. Makes 4 servings.

Variation: Place Boursin cheese in center of thinly pounded chicken breast. Wrap chicken around cheese and secure at top and sides with toothpicks. Bread and bake as above. Top each breast with 1/4 cup crushed fruit.

BERRY MINI MEAT LOAVES

1 1/4 pounds lean ground beef
1 cup CRAN•FRUIT™ crushed fruit
1 egg
1 small onion, finely chopped
2 tablespoons bread crumbs
3/4 teaspoon pepper

Preheat oven to 350 degrees.

Combine all ingredients in a medium mixing bowl. Divide meat evenly into a 12-cup muffin pan, mounding slightly.

Place muffin pan on a baking sheet. Bake 25 minutes; tip muffin pan slightly to drain fat. Return to oven and bake 10 minutes or until done. Makes 12 mini loaves.

ZESTY JOES

1 pound ground beef
1/2 cup ketchup
1 tablespoon chili powder
3/4 cup CRAN•FRUIT™ crushed fruit
5 hamburger buns

Brown hamburger in a medium-sized skillet. Drain fat. Add remaining ingredients and heat through. Serve on buns. Makes 5 servings.

CHICKEN MELT

2 whole boneless, skinless chicken breasts
Oil
Charcoal seasoning or pepper
3/4 cup CRAN•FRUIT™ crushed fruit
1 small apple, thinly sliced
4 thin slices cheddar cheese

Separate chicken breasts. Brush with oil; season with charcoal seasoning or pepper to taste. Grill or broil chicken until no longer pink inside. Spread each breast with 3 tablespoons of crushed fruit. Place apple slices on each breast, and top with a cheddar cheese slice. Cook until cheese has melted. Makes 4 servings.

"*These berries soon will grace*
a festive board,

Will add a zest to meals and
make them gay,

And they will bring back
memories of the scene,

At cranberry picking time,
down Cape Cod way!"

—*from "Cranberry Picking Time*
on Cape Cod" by Grace Sewell Winslow

CHOCOLATE CRANBERRY DESSERT SAUCE

1 16-ounce can OCEAN SPRAY® jellied cranberry sauce
1/2 cup semi-sweet chocolate bits

Combine cranberry sauce and chocolate bits in a medium saucepan. Melt over medium heat, whisking occasionally until smooth. Cool. Serve over desserts, ice cream, crepes, etc. Makes 2 cups.

SESAME HONEY GLAZE

1 8-ounce can OCEAN SPRAY® jellied cranberry sauce
2 tablespoons honey
1 tablespoon soy sauce
2 tablespoons sesame seeds
Dash ginger

Combine ingredients in a small saucepan. Cook over medium heat just until sauce is smooth, whisking frequently. Liberally brush on poultry during cooking. Makes 1 cup.

CHAPTER 7

MAIN MEALS

SPICY CRANBERRY PORK

1 16-ounce can OCEAN SPRAY® whole berry
   cranberry sauce
1/2 cup raisins
1/2 cup peeled, diced apple
1/4 cup + 2 tablespoons sugar
1/4 cup + 2 tablespoons vinegar
1/8 teaspoon allspice
1/8 teaspoon ginger
1/8 teaspoon cinnamon
Dash ground cloves
4 boneless pork loin chops

Preheat oven to 350 degrees.

Combine all ingredients, except pork, in a medium saucepan. Cook on medium heat, stirring occasionally, until apples are tender and sauce has thickened slightly. Keep warm until serving time.

Bake pork loin chops for 15 minutes. Top each loin with 1/4 cup sauce. Bake for another 10 minutes or until internal temperature reaches 160 degrees on a meat thermometer. Spoon on extra sauce before serving. Makes 4 servings.

TIP: Pork loin chops can also be prepared on the grill.

BEST BBQ CHICKEN

1 15-ounce can tomato sauce
3/4 cup CRAN•FRUIT™ crushed fruit
3 tablespoons brown sugar
3 tablespoons Worcestershire sauce
1 teaspoon chili powder
1/3 cup vinegar
4 chicken breasts

Preheat oven to 375 degrees.

Combine all ingredients, except chicken, in a medium saucepan. Heat sauce to boiling. Reduce heat and simmer for 15 minutes, stirring occasionally. Arrange chicken in a 13x9-inch baking pan.

Bake for 30 minutes. Brush or pour sauce over chicken. Bake 1 hour or until thoroughly done, basting throughout cooking. Makes 4 servings.

MAPLE GLAZED CHICKEN

4 chicken legs
8 slices bacon
1 cup CRAN•FRUIT™ cranberry raspberry or
   cranberry strawberry crushed fruit
1/2 cup maple syrup

Preheat oven to 350 degrees.

Microwave bacon for 4 minutes on HIGH or until bacon is partially cooked. Wrap 2 strips of bacon around each chicken leg. Place in a large baking pan.

Combine crushed fruit and maple syrup. Brush glaze on chicken.

Bake chicken for 1 hour 15 minutes or until chicken is no longer pink inside, brushing frequently with glaze. Makes 4 servings.

PRECEDING: SPICY CRANBERRY PORK. LEFT: A SKILLED HARVESTER COULD GATHER 200 POUNDS OF CRANBERRIES IN AN HOUR USING THE HAND SCOOP.

TURKEY FAJITAS WITH SOUTHWESTERN CRANBERRY SAUCE

SAUCE:
1 1/2 cups OCEAN SPRAY® whole berry
    cranberry sauce
1 green onion, white and green parts, sliced
1 teaspoon dried cilantro
1 teaspoon cumin
1/4 cup chopped canned jalapeño peppers
1 teaspoon lime juice

FAJITAS:
1/4 cup vegetable oil
4 green peppers, cut into 1/2-inch strips
2 large onions, sliced
3 large garlic cloves, minced
2 teaspoons dried cilantro
1 teaspoon cumin
3 cups diced cooked turkey
8 flour tortillas, heated

TO MAKE SOUTHWESTERN
CRANBERRY SAUCE:
Thoroughly combine all sauce ingredients in a
medium mixing bowl. Set aside until serving time.

TO MAKE TURKEY FAJITAS:
Heat oil in a large skillet. Add peppers, onion,
garlic, cilantro and cumin. Cook until peppers are
almost tender, stirring constantly. Add turkey.
Cook until turkey is heated through.

TO SERVE:
Place turkey mixture in the center of a tortilla.
Spoon on some cranberry sauce. Fold sides of
tortilla over filling. Makes 4 servings.

CRANBERRY CHICKEN MARGARITA

6 boneless, skinless chicken breast halves
2 tablespoons olive oil
Coarse salt
1 small garlic clove, minced
1 cup OCEAN SPRAY® whole berry
    cranberry sauce
3 tablespoons tequila
1 teaspoon lime juice
1 1/2 tablespoons chopped cilantro
Lime wedges

Slice breasts in half horizontally. Pound with a
meat mallet or rolling pin to about 3/8-inch
thickness.

Heat oil in a large skillet over medium heat.
Add chicken and cook until lightly browned, about
3 minutes per side. Remove chicken to a warm
serving platter and sprinkle lightly with coarse
salt. Cover loosely with foil; keep warm until serving time.

Add garlic to skillet and cook over low heat 1
minute. Stir in cranberry sauce and tequila; bring
to a boil. Reduce heat. Simmer 5 minutes or until
sauce is thickened, stirring occasionally. Stir in
lime juice and cilantro.

Spoon some of the sauce over chicken.
Sprinkle with additional cilantro, if desired. Serve
immediately with remaining sauce, lime wedges
and coarse salt. Makes 6 servings.

GINGERBREAD PANCAKES WITH CRANBERRY ORANGE SYRUP

1 cup corn syrup
1/4 cup thawed orange juice concentrate
1/4 cup CRAN•FRUIT™ cranberry orange crushed fruit
1 cup flour
2 1/2 teaspoons cinnamon
1 1/2 teaspoons ginger
1 teaspoon baking powder
1/2 teaspoon baking soda
1/2 cup milk
1/2 cup molasses
1 egg
2 tablespoons oil

TO MAKE SYRUP:

Combine corn syrup, concentrate and crushed fruit in a medium saucepan; bring to a boil. Reduce heat and simmer for 3 minutes without stirring. Watch carefully to prevent syrup from foaming over. Remove from heat. Chill to thicken. Serve at room temperature or warm.

TO MAKE PANCAKES:

Combine dry ingredients in a medium mixing bowl. Combine liquid ingredients in a separate bowl. Add to dry ingredients, mixing just until the dry ingredients are moist.

Spoon about 1/4 cup batter for each pancake onto a lightly greased skillet. Cook until lightly browned on both sides. Turn pancake when surface bubbles and underside is lightly browned. Makes about 3 servings.

HARVEST OVEN PANCAKE

BATTER:
1/2 cup flour
2 tablespoons sugar
1/2 cup milk
1 egg

FILLING:
1 1/4 cups OCEAN SPRAY® fresh or frozen cranberries
2 apples, diced
1/2 cup brown sugar
1/2 cup chopped walnuts
1/4 cup butter or margarine
1 teaspoon cinnamon
1/2 teaspoon nutmeg

Preheat oven to 400 degrees. Grease a 9-inch pie plate.

Combine all batter ingredients in a medium mixing bowl. Beat using an electric mixer for one minute. Pour batter into prepared pan. Bake for 20 minutes or until golden brown.

Cook all filling ingredients in a skillet until cranberries and apples have softened.

Remove pancake from oven. If center has puffed, place a clean potholder or dishtowel on top and gently push down. Spoon filling into center of pancake. Serve immediately. Makes 4 servings.

OPPOSITE: BRIMMING WITH FRUIT AND FRESH FROM THE OVEN, THE HARVEST OVEN PANCAKE IS HEARTY ENOUGH FOR BREAKFAST, LUNCH OR DINNER.

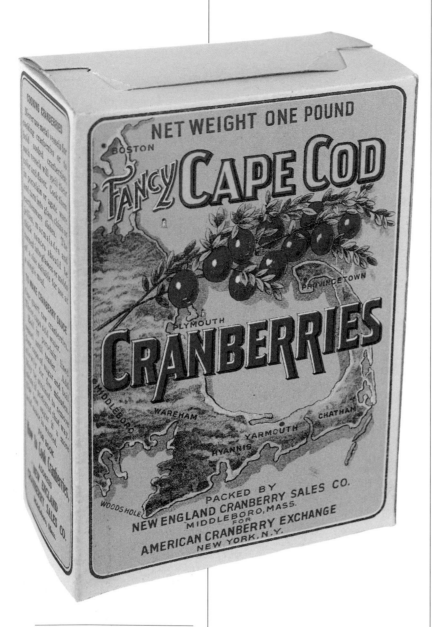

CRANBERRIES WERE SOLD TO CONSUMERS IN ONE-POUND BOXES AT THE TURN OF THE CENTURY.

CRUNCHY STUFFED FRENCH TOAST

- 6 cups corn flakes
- 1 16-ounce loaf Italian bread
- 1 cup milk
- 2 eggs
- 1 teaspoon cinnamon
- 1/2 teaspoon nutmeg
- 1 16-ounce can OCEAN SPRAY® whole berry cranberry sauce
- 1 1/4 teaspoons almond extract
- Butter

Place corn flakes in a food processor and process into crumbs. Cut bread into 11 1-inch slices. Make a pocket in each slice by cutting through the top crust almost to the bottom crust. Combine milk, eggs and spices in a medium mixing bowl.

Combine cranberry sauce and almond extract in a small mixing bowl. Spread about 3 tablespoons of cranberry sauce mixture in each bread pocket. Dip each slice in milk mixture; then roll in corn flake crumbs, coating thoroughly.

Heat a small amount of butter in a large skillet. Cook a few slices at a time until golden brown on both sides and heated through. Serve with maple syrup. Makes 11 servings.

PECAN BREADED PORK WITH CRANBERRY APRICOT SAUCE

1 pound boneless pork loin
1 egg
2 cups finely chopped pecans
2 1/2 cups OCEAN SPRAY® fresh or frozen
   cranberries
1/2 cup water
1/2 cup sugar
3/4 cup apricot jam
Oil

Trim fat off pork. Cut each loin in half horizontally, forming 2 1/2-inch thick slices. Pound each piece to 1/4-inch thick.

Beat egg with 2 tablespoons water. Dip each piece of pork into egg, then lightly coat with pecans, pressing to stick, if necessary. Set aside.

Bring cranberries, water and sugar to a boil in a medium saucepan. Cook until berries pop. Place a wire mesh strainer over a medium mixing bowl. Pour contents of saucepan into strainer. Press cranberries with the back of a spoon, frequently scraping the outside of the strainer, until no pulp is left. Stir contents of bowl.

Return puree to saucepan. Add jam and heat until jam is combined, stirring occasionally. Keep sauce warm until serving time.

Heat 1/4 cup oil in a skillet. Fry pork 2-3 minutes on each side or until pork is golden brown and cooked throughout.

Transfer pork to a serving platter. Pour some sauce over pork and serve extra sauce on the side. Makes 4–6 servings.

MY "OUT-OF-THIS-WORLD" FIERY FRUITED CHILI

1/4 cup vegetable oil
2 pound mixture of lean cubed beef, pork
   and lamb
1 16-ounce package frozen chopped onions
2 16-ounce cans tomatoes, drained
2 6-ounce cans tomato paste
1/4 cup chili powder
1 envelope Italian salad dressing mix
1 4-ounce can hot chilies, chopped
2 16-ounce cans red kidney beans, drained
2 teaspoons cumin
1 32-ounce bottle CRANAPPLE® cranberry
   apple juice drink, reserving 3 tablespoons
1 8-ounce package cream cheese, softened
1 3-ounce package cream cheese, softened
1 cup halved green grapes
2 tablespoons chopped maraschino cherries
Toasted rye bread triangles
1 20-ounce can pineapple chunks

Heat oil in a Dutch oven or large pot. Add meat and brown on all sides. Remove from pan and set aside. Add onion to pot. Cook until the onions become translucent, about 5 minutes. Return meat to pot. Add tomatoes, tomato paste, chili powder, salad dressing mix, chilies, kidney beans, cumin and cranberry apple juice drink. Cover and cook for 1 1/2 hours over medium-low heat, stirring occasionally.

Meanwhile, combine both packages of cream cheese with enough of the reserved cranberry apple drink to make spreading consistency. Add grapes and cherries; mix well. Spread on rye triangles. Set aside until serving time.

Add pineapple chunks and juice to chili. Bring to a boil. Serve with rye triangles. Makes 8 servings.

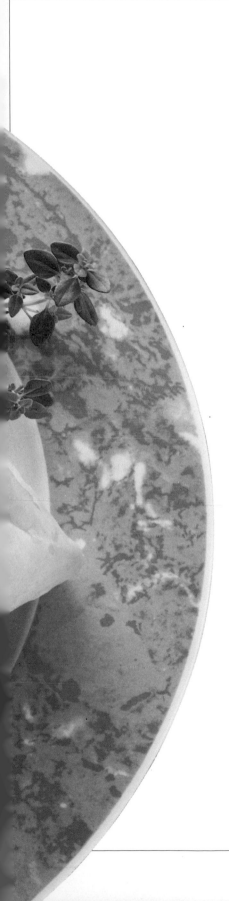

WILD RICE AND CRANBERRY PHYLLO ROLLS

....

16 sheets phyllo dough
Butter or margarine, melted
2 cups cooked long grain and
  wild rice
2 whole boneless chicken
  breasts, halved, cooked
2 1/2 cups OCEAN SPRAY®
  whole berry cranberry sauce

Preheat oven to 350 degrees.

Using 2 sheets of phyllo at a time, lay phyllo on work surface and brush with butter. Top with another 2 sheets of phyllo and brush with butter.

Working at the short end of the phyllo, place 1/2 cup of rice on the lower third of the dough. Top rice with a chicken breast half. Spoon 1/4 cup of cranberry sauce on top of chicken.

Fold the long sides and bottom of dough into center. Roll up jelly-roll style and place in a baking pan, sauce side up. Brush with butter.

Bake until phyllo is golden brown and center is heated through, about 30 minutes. Heat remaining cranberry sauce and spoon on top of rolls before serving. Makes 4 generous servings.

_WILD RICE AND CRANBERRY
PHYLLO ROLLS MAKE AN ELEGANT
DINNER PARTY ENTRÉE._

CRANBERRY CHICKEN MUFFULETTA

....

1 9-inch round pumpernickel
  bread
1 12-ounce package
  CRAN•FRUIT™ crushed fruit
5 garlic cloves, finely minced
2 tablespoons coarsely chopped
  fresh basil
6 thin slices red onion
1 cup shredded Monterey Jack
  cheese
1 1/4 cups cooked chicken, cut
  into 1/2-inch pieces

Preheat oven to 350 degrees.

Slice the top quarter off of the bread. Hollow out bottom and top of the bread, leaving 1/2-inch shell. Use the bread you pull out for croutons or bread crumbs. Set hollowed-out bread shell aside.

Combine crushed fruit, garlic and basil in a small mixing bowl. Spread in bottom and top of bread. Place 3 slices of onion in bottom of bread. Top with 1/2 cup of cheese. Add chicken. Spread remaining cheese over chicken and top with remaining onion. Place top on bread.

Wrap loaf in foil. Bake for 30 minutes or until heated through. Remove from oven and let sit for about 5 minutes. Cut into wedges and serve. Makes 4–6 servings.

Breakfast Tortillas

1/2 pound ground sausage meat
1 cup OCEAN SPRAY® fresh or frozen
    cranberries, coarsely chopped
1/3 cup chopped onion
1/3 cup chopped green pepper
Shredded Monterey Jack Cheese
3 8-inch flour tortillas

Lightly brown sausage meat in a medium skillet over medium heat. Add cranberries, onion and green pepper. Continue cooking until sausage is cooked and onions are tender. Sprinkle cheese over top of meat; cook until melted. Distribute evenly down the middle of each tortilla. Fold sides of tortilla over filling. Makes 3 servings.

New England Cornbread Stuffing

2 cups cornbread stuffing
1/2 pound sausage meat, cooked, drained
    and crumbled
3/4 cup CRAISINS™ sweetened dried cranberries
1/3 cup chopped pecans
1 teaspoon thyme
1/2 cup chicken broth

Preheat oven to 350 degrees.

Combine all ingredients, except chicken broth, in a medium casserole dish. Add chicken broth; mix well. Add more chicken broth for a moister stuffing.

Cover and bake for 30 minutes or until heated through. Makes about 3 cups.

Savory Cranberry Turkey Casserole

2 cups cooked turkey, cut into 1/2-inch cubes
1 cup onion, finely diced
1 teaspoon thyme
1 cup OCEAN SPRAY® jellied cranberry sauce
1 cup baking mix
1 cup milk
2 eggs

Preheat oven to 400 degrees. Grease a 9 1/4-inch quiche pan.

Combine turkey, onion and thyme. Spread evenly on bottom of pan. Break up cranberry sauce with a fork until smooth. Spoon by teaspoonfuls randomly over turkey.

Combine baking mix, milk and eggs in a blender. Blend on high speed for 1 minute. Pour over casserole.

Bake for 30 minutes or until a toothpick inserted into the center comes out clean. Makes 8–10 servings.

AN EARLY BRAND OF CRANBERRY SAUCE. (LABEL, CIRCA 1920s)

CRANBERRY COUNTRY STYLE RIBS

2 pounds boneless country style pork ribs

PUREE:
2 1/2 cups OCEAN SPRAY® fresh or frozen
   cranberries
1/2 cup water
1/2 cup sugar

SAUCE:
1 recipe cranberry puree
1 cup brown sugar
1/2 cup chili sauce
1/4 cup + 2 tablespoons vinegar
1/4 cup chopped onion
1/4 cup Lea & Perrins Worcestershire sauce

Preheat oven to 350 degrees. Bake ribs until halfway done, approximately 30 minutes. Meanwhile, prepare puree and sauce.

TO PREPARE PUREE:
Bring all puree ingredients to a boil in a medium saucepan. Cook until cranberries pop. Place a wire mesh strainer over a medium mixing bowl. Pour contents of saucepan into strainer. Press cranberries with the back of a spoon, frequently scraping the outside of the strainer until no pulp is left. Stir contents of bowl.

TO PREPARE SAUCE:
Combine all sauce ingredients in a medium saucepan and bring to a boil. Reduce heat and simmer until sauce thickens, about 20 minutes, stirring frequently.
   Drain partially baked ribs. Pour sauce over ribs and bake until pork is no longer pink, about 15 minutes. Makes 4 servings.

CRANBERRY APPLE CHICKEN BREASTS

1 1/4 cups coarsely chopped OCEAN SPRAY®
   fresh or frozen cranberries
1/3 cup +2 tablespoons diced apples
1/4 cup +2 teaspoons chopped walnuts
4 boneless skinless chicken breasts, pounded to
   1/2-inch thick
1 cup grated Monterey Jack cheese

Preheat oven to 350 degrees.
   Combine chopped cranberries, diced apples and walnuts in a medium glass bowl.
   Place breasts in a 13x9-inch baking pan. Top each breast with 1/3 cup of filling. Bake for 30 minutes or until chicken is no longer pink inside. Top each breast with 1/4 cup cheese. Bake for an additional 5 minutes or until cheese has melted. Makes 4 servings.

ONE POUND BOXES CONTINUED TO BE THE PREFERRED SIZE AND PACKAGE TYPE FOR CONSUMERS. (BOX, CIRCA MID-1950S)

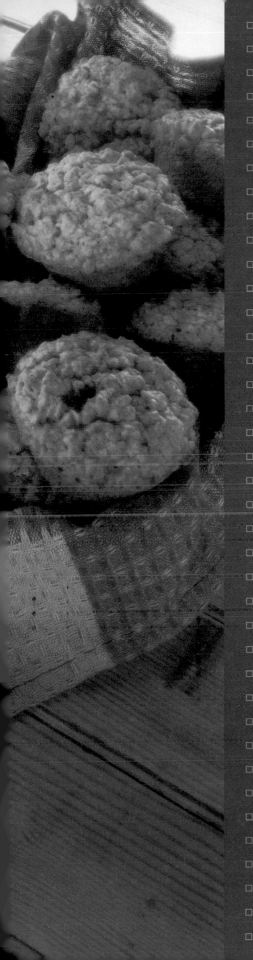

CHAPTER 8

BREADS & MUFFINS

CRANBERRY STREUSEL MUFFINS

STREUSEL:
1/2 cup brown sugar
1/2 cup flour
2 teaspoons cinnamon
1/4 cup softened butter

BATTER:
2 cups flour
1/2 cup sugar
2 teaspoons baking powder
1 teaspoon salt
1 cup OCEAN SPRAY® fresh or frozen
   cranberries, coarsely chopped
1/2 cup chopped walnuts
1 egg
1/2 cup melted butter
1/2 cup milk

Preheat oven to 350 degrees. Grease a 12-cup muffin tin.

Place streusel ingredients in a small mixing bowl. Work butter into dry ingredients until butter is the size of small peas using a pastry blender or fork. Set aside.

Combine flour, sugar, baking powder and salt in a medium mixing bowl. Stir in cranberries and walnuts. Combine remaining ingredients in a separate mixing bowl. Add to dry ingredients, mixing just until the dry ingredients are moist.

Fill each muffin cup 2/3 full with batter. Sprinkle streusel over tops. Bake for 25–30 minutes or until golden brown. Remove from tins; cool on a wire rack. Makes 12 muffins.

CRANBERRY APPLE WHEEL

3-4 cups flour
1 package yeast
1/3 cup sugar
1/2 teaspoon salt
1/3 cup butter, melted
1 cup milk
1 egg
1 cup coarsely chopped OCEAN SPRAY®
   fresh or frozen cranberries
2 apples, peeled and diced
1/2 cup chopped walnuts
1/2 cup brown sugar
1 teaspoon cinnamon
1/2 teaspoon nutmeg
5 tablespoons flour
1 cup powdered sugar
2 tablespoons water

Combine 2 cups flour, yeast, sugar and salt in a medium mixing bowl. Combine butter and milk; heat to a temperature of 120–130 degrees. Add to dry ingredients, mixing thoroughly. Add egg; mix well. Add enough of remaining flour to make a soft dough that is not sticky when handled.

Lightly grease a medium mixing bowl. Place dough in bowl and roll around so that it is lightly covered with grease. Place bowl with dough in a warm place until it has doubled in size.

Meanwhile, combine remaining ingredients, except powdered sugar and water, in a medium mixing bowl. Punch down dough and place on a cookie sheet. Flatten dough into a 10-inch circle. Spread topping over dough, leaving an inch all around. Place in a warm place until dough has doubled in size.

Preheat oven to 350 degrees. Bake for approximately 30 minutes or until crust is golden brown. Combine powdered sugar and water in a small mixing bowl to make glaze. Cool wheel completely and drizzle with glaze. Makes 1 10-inch wheel.

PRECEDING: CRANBERRY APPLE WHEEL

CRANBERRY PUMPKIN MUFFINS

2 cups flour
1/2 cup brown sugar
1 teaspoon baking soda
1 teaspoon cinnamon
1/2 teaspoon nutmeg
1/2 teaspoon salt
1 cup pumpkin
2 cups OCEAN SPRAY® fresh or frozen
   cranberries, coarsely chopped
1/2 cup oil
1/4 cup milk
1/4 cup molasses
1 egg

Preheat oven to 350 degrees. Grease muffin tins.

Combine dry ingredients in a medium mixing bowl. Combine remaining ingredients in a separate mixing bowl. Add liquid ingredients to dry, mixing just until the dry ingredients are moist.

Fill each muffin cup 2/3 full with batter. Bake for 30 minutes or until golden brown. Remove from tins; cool on a wire rack. Makes about 12 muffins.

CRANBERRY MUFFINS

1 1/4 cups sugar
1/4 cup butter or margarine, softened
2 eggs
2 cups flour
2 teaspoons baking powder
1/4 teaspoon salt
1/2 cup milk
1/2 cup chopped walnuts
2 cups OCEAN SPRAY® fresh or frozen
   cranberries, coarsely chopped

Preheat oven to 350 degrees.

Mix sugar and butter together in a medium mixing bowl until completely blended. Add eggs one at a time, beating after each addition.

Stir together flour, baking powder and salt in a separate medium mixing bowl. Add this alternately with the milk to the butter mixture. Stir in nuts and cranberries.

Spoon into 12 paper-lined muffin cups, filling 3/4 full with batter. Bake 25–30 minutes or until golden brown. Makes 12 muffins.

Muffins. Cut our sauce into small cubes and mix in your favorite batter. Delicious in Bran or dark muffins.

CRANBERRIES AND MUFFINS: A TRIED AND TRUE COMBINATION. (LABEL, CIRCA 1920S)

CRANBERRY COFFEE BRAID.

CRANBERRY COFFEE BRAID

....

1 loaf frozen bread dough, thawed
1 12-ounce package CRAN•FRUIT™ crushed fruit, drained
1/2 cup chopped walnuts
1 teaspoon cinnamon
1 cup powdered sugar
2 tablespoons water

Roll dough out into an 11x15-inch rectangle on a lightly floured surface. Place on a cookie sheet. Combine crushed fruit, nuts and cinnamon in a small mixing bowl. Spread lengthwise down the center of dough in a 4-inch wide strip.

Cut dough on either side of filling into 1-inch wide strips. Fold dough strips alternately across center of filling. Let rise in a warm place for 30 minutes.

Preheat oven to 375 degrees. Bake braid for 30 minutes or until golden brown. Cool completely. Combine powdered sugar and water in a small mixing bowl. Drizzle on braid. Best if served same day. Makes 1 braid.

HEARTY OATMEAL CRANBERRY MUFFINS

....

2 cups old-fashioned oats
1 cup baking mix
1/2 cup brown sugar
2 teaspoons cinnamon
1 egg
1/4 cup oil
1/2 cup milk
1/2 cup OCEAN SPRAY® jellied cranberry sauce

Preheat oven to 375 degrees. Grease a 6-cup muffin tin.

Combine oats, baking mix, brown sugar and cinnamon in a medium mixing bowl. Combine egg, oil and milk in a separate mixing bowl. Add to dry ingredients, mixing just until the dry ingredients are moist.

Fill each muffin cup 1/3 full with batter. Spoon about 1/2 tablespoon cranberry sauce into the center of each cup. Top with enough batter to cover sauce.

Bake for 22 minutes or until golden brown. Cool slightly and remove from pan. Makes 6 muffins.

Quick, easy & good!

CRANBERRY ALMOND BREAD.

CRANBERRY ALMOND BREAD

2 cups flour
1/2 cup sugar
2 teaspoons baking powder
1 teaspoon salt
1 egg
1/4 cup milk
1/2 cup butter, melted
2 teaspoons almond extract
1 1/2 cups OCEAN SPRAY® fresh or frozen
    cranberries
1 tablespoon sugar
1/4 cup sliced almonds

Preheat oven to 375 degrees. Grease an 8 1/2 x 4 1/2 x 2 1/2-inch loaf pan.

Combine flour, sugar, baking powder and salt in a medium mixing bowl. Combine egg, milk, butter and almond extract in a separate mixing bowl. Add to dry ingredients, mixing just until moist. Stir in cranberries.

Spread batter in loaf pan. Sprinkle with sugar and almonds. Bake for 45 minutes. Reduce heat to 350 degrees. Bake for 30 minutes or until a toothpick inserted in center of loaf comes out clean. Makes 1 loaf.

CRANBERRY BLUEBERRY MUFFINS

2 cups flour
1/2 cup sugar
2 teaspoons baking powder
1 teaspoon salt
1 egg
1 cup milk
1/2 cup oil
1/2 cup OCEAN SPRAY® fresh or frozen
    cranberries
1/2 cup wild blueberries
Sugar

Preheat oven to 350 degrees. Grease a 12-cup muffin tin.

Combine flour, sugar, baking powder and salt in a medium mixing bowl. Combine egg, milk and oil in a small mixing bowl. Add liquid ingredients to dry, stirring just until dry ingredients are moist. Stir in cranberries and blueberries.

Fill muffin cups 2/3 full with batter. Sprinkle tops of muffins with sugar. Bake for about 25 minutes or until golden brown. Cool 5 minutes in the pan; remove and cool completely on a wire rack. Makes 12 muffins.

MICROWAVE CRANBERRY CRUMB CAKE

2 cups flour
3/4 cup brown sugar
1 1/2 teaspoons baking powder
1/2 teaspoon salt
1 teaspoon cinnamon
1/2 cup butter or margarine, softened
1/3 cup milk
1 egg
1 teaspoon vanilla
1 cup OCEAN SPRAY® whole berry cranberry sauce
1/2 cup sugar
1/3 cup flour
3/4 teaspoon cinnamon
1/4 cup butter or margarine

In a medium mixing bowl using an electric mixer, combine flour, brown sugar, baking powder, salt, cinnamon and butter. Add milk, egg, vanilla and cranberry sauce; mix well. Spread batter evenly in an 8-inch round ungreased microwave safe baking dish.

Using an electric mixer, thoroughly combine sugar, flour, cinnamon and butter or margarine in a small mixing bowl. Sprinkle evenly over batter.

Microwave on 70% power for 15 minutes. Let stand, covered with waxed paper, for 15 minutes. Let cool for at least 30 minutes before serving. Makes 1 coffeecake.

CRANBERRY BANANA BREAD

1 cup sugar
1/2 cup butter or margarine, softened
1 cup mashed banana
1/4 cup milk
2 eggs
2 cups flour
2 teaspoons baking powder
1/2 cups chopped walnuts
1 1/2 cups coarsely chopped OCEAN SPRAY® fresh or frozen cranberries

Preheat oven to 350 degrees. Grease an 8 1/2 x 4 1/2 x 2 1/2-inch loaf pan.

Mix sugar and butter together in a medium mixing bowl until completely blended. Add banana, milk and eggs, mixing well. Add dry ingredients, mixing just until moist. Stir in nuts and cranberries.

Spread batter evenly in a loaf pan. Bake for 1 hour and 10 minutes or until a toothpick inserted into the center of the bread comes out clean. Remove from pan and cool completely on a wire rack. Makes 1 loaf.

CRANBERRY LEMON-YOGURT BREAD

2 cups flour
2 teaspoons baking powder
3/4 teaspoon salt
1/2 teaspoon baking soda
1/4 cup butter or margarine, softened
3/4 cup sugar
1 cup plain, low-fat yogurt
2 eggs
1/4 cup lemon juice
1 cup OCEAN SPRAY® fresh or frozen cranberries, coarsely chopped
Zest of 1 lemon

GLAZE:
1/2 cup powdered sugar
1/2 teaspoon lemon zest
2 tablespoons lemon juice

Preheat oven to 350 degrees. Grease and flour a 9 x 5-inch loaf pan. Combine flour, baking powder, salt and baking soda in a large bowl; set aside.

Using an electric mixer, beat butter or margarine and sugar in a medium mixing bowl until light and fluffy. Add yogurt, eggs and lemon juice; mix well. Next, add cranberries and lemon zest. Add cranberry mixture to dry ingredients, mixing just until dry ingredients are moist.

Spread batter evenly in pan. Bake 50 minutes or until a toothpick inserted into the center of the bread comes out clean. Cool in pan 10 minutes. Remove from pan. Cool completely on a wire rack. Makes 1 loaf.

CRANBERRY BANANA NUT SCONES

- 2 1/2 cups flour
- 1/2 cup brown sugar
- 2 teaspoons baking powder
- 1 1/2 teaspoons nutmeg
- 1 teaspoon salt
- 1/2 cup butter or margarine, softened
- 2 cups OCEAN SPRAY® fresh or frozen cranberries, coarsely chopped
- 3 ripe bananas, mashed
- 1/2 cup chopped walnuts
- 1 egg

Preheat oven to 350 degrees.

Combine dry ingredients in a medium mixing bowl. Work butter or margarine into dry ingredients until butter is the size of small peas using a pastry blender or fork.

Combine cranberries, bananas, walnuts and egg in a medium mixing bowl. Add to dry ingredients, mixing thoroughly.

Spread dough into a 10-inch circle on an ungreased cookie sheet. Cut into 8 wedges. Bake for 25 minutes or until golden brown. Remove scones from oven and re-cut wedges. Serve warm. Makes 8 scones.

CRANBERRIES AND BANANAS ADD A TWIST TO THE TRADITIONAL TEA-TIME SCONE.

CRANBERRY STRUDEL

1 17 1/4-ounce package frozen puff pastry
2 cups coarsely chopped OCEAN SPRAY® fresh or frozen cranberries
1 cup raisins
1/2 cup chopped walnuts
1 apple, peeled and diced
1/3 cup brown sugar
1/2 teaspoon cinnamon
1/2 teaspoon nutmeg
1/2 teaspoon allspice
1/4 cup flour

Preheat oven to 350 degrees. Thaw pastry according to package directions.

Place thawed pastry on cookie sheets. Combine remaining ingredients in a medium mixing bowl. Divide the filling between the two sheets of pastry. Spread filling lengthwise down the center of pastry in a 3-inch wide strip.

Cut dough on either side of filling into 1-inch wide strips. Fold dough strips alternately across center of filling. Bake for 30 minutes or until golden brown. Makes 2 strudels.

CRANBERRY ORANGE SCONES

1 1/2 cups flour
3 tablespoons sugar
2 teaspoons baking powder
Dash salt
1/4 cup butter, softened
1/3 cup vanilla yogurt
1 egg
2/3 cup OCEAN SPRAY® fresh or frozen cranberries, coarsely chopped
Zest of 1 orange

Preheat oven to 400 degrees. Lightly grease a cookie sheet.

Combine flour, sugar, baking powder and salt in a large mixing bowl. Work butter into dry ingredients, using a pastry blender or fork, until butter is the size of small peas.

Combine yogurt and egg in a small mixing bowl. Add cranberries and orange zest. Add to dry ingredients, mixing with a fork just until the dry ingredients are moist.

Knead dough on a lightly floured surface until dough is almost smooth. Cut dough in half. Shape each half into a 4-inch circle and place on cookie sheet. Cut each circle into 6 wedges. (Do not separate wedges.)

Bake for 15 minutes or until golden brown. Cool 5 minutes on a cooling rack. Sprinkle with powdered sugar, if desired. Cut wedges and serve warm. Makes 12 scones.

CRANBERRY APPLE BREAD

2 cups peeled, chopped apple
3/4 cup sugar
2 tablespoons oil
1 egg
1 1/2 cups flour
1 1/2 teaspoons baking powder
1/2 teaspoon baking soda
1 teaspoon cinnamon
1 cup OCEAN SPRAY® fresh or frozen cranberries
1/2 cup chopped walnuts

Preheat oven to 350 degrees. Grease an 8 1/2 x 4 1/2 x 2-inch loaf pan.

Combine apples, sugar and oil in a medium mixing bowl. Add egg, mixing well. Combine dry ingredients in a separate mixing bowl. Add to apple mixture, mixing just until the dry ingredients are moist. Stir in cranberries and walnuts.

Spread batter evenly in loaf pan. Bake for 1 hour or until a toothpick inserted into the center of the bread comes out clean. Makes 1 loaf.

CRANBERRY YOGURT COFFEE CAKE

1 18 1/2-ounce package
   yellow cake mix
1 3 3/4-ounce package vanilla
   instant pudding mix
4 eggs
1 cup plain yogurt
1/4 cup vegetable oil
1 16-ounce can OCEAN
   SPRAY® whole berry
   cranberry sauce
1/2 cup chopped walnuts

Preheat oven to 350 degrees.
Generously grease and lightly
flour a 9x13x2-inch pan.

Combine cake mix, pudding
mix, eggs, yogurt and oil in a
large mixing bowl. Beat with
electric mixer on high for 3
minutes. Scrape bowl often.

Spread 2/3 of batter in prepared pan. Spoon cranberry
sauce evenly over it. Spoon
remaining batter evenly
over cranberry
sauce. Sprinkle
with nuts.

Bake 55 to 60
minutes. Cool on a
wire rack 35 min-
utes. Makes 20
servings.

CRANBERRY MEDLEY BREAD

2 1/2 cups baking mix
3/4 cup brown sugar
2 teaspoons cinnamon
2 teaspoons baking powder
2 cups OCEAN SPRAY® fresh
   or frozen cranberries
1 20-ounce can crushed
   pineapple, drained
1 cup shredded carrot,
   loosely packed
1 egg

Preheat oven to 375 degrees.
Grease one 9x5x3-inch loaf pan.

Combine baking mix, brown
sugar, cinnamon and baking
powder. Set aside. Combine
cranberries, pineapple, carrot
and egg. Add to dry ingredients, mixing just until the dry
ingredients are moist. Spread
batter evenly in loaf pan.

Bake for 1 hour or until a
toothpick inserted into the center comes out clean. Remove
from pan and cool com-
pletely on a wire
rack. Makes 1 loaf.

*CANNING CRANBERRIES
EXTENDED THEIR USAGE
THROUGHOUT THE YEAR.
(CAN, CIRCA 1940s)*

CRANBERRY CAPPUCCINO MUFFINS

1 3/4 cups flour
2/3 cup sugar
1 1/2 teaspoons baking
   powder
1/2 teaspoon baking soda
3 tablespoons cocoa
1 tablespoon instant coffee
1/2 teaspoon cinnamon
3/4 teaspoon salt
3/4 cup milk
1 egg
6 tablespoons oil
1 1/4 cups coarsely chopped
   OCEAN SPRAY® fresh or
   frozen cranberries

Preheat oven to 375 degrees.
Grease muffin tins.

Combine dry ingredients in
a medium mixing bowl.
Combine remaining ingredients,
except cranberries, in a separate mixing bowl. Add liquid
ingredients to dry, mixing just
until all the dry ingredients are
moist. Stir in cranberries.

Fill muffin cups 2/3 of the
way full with batter. Bake 25
minutes or until muffins test
done. Makes 1 dozen muffins.

CRANBERRY NUT TEA RING

....

DOUGH:
3-4 cups flour
1 package yeast
1/3 cup sugar
1/2 teaspoon salt
1/3 cup butter, melted
1 cup milk
1 egg

GLAZE:
1 cup powdered sugar
2 tablespoons water

FILLING:
1 cup coarsely
  chopped OCEAN
  SPRAY® fresh
  or frozen
  cranberries
1/2 cup chopped
  walnuts
1/2 cup brown
  sugar
1/2 teaspoon
  nutmeg
5 tablespoons flour

To make the dough, combine 2 cups flour, yeast, sugar and salt in a medium mixing bowl. Combine butter and milk and heat to a temperature of 120 degrees to 130 degrees. Add to dry ingredients; mixing thoroughly. Add egg; mix well. Add enough of remaining flour to make a soft dough that is not sticky when handled.

Lightly grease a medium mixing bowl. Place dough in bowl and roll around so that it is lightly covered with grease. Place bowl with dough in a warm place until dough has doubled in size.

Preheat oven to 350 degrees.

Combine filling ingredients in a medium mixing bowl. Punch dough down and roll into a 12 x 24-inch rectangle. Spread filling over dough, leaving an inch all around. Roll jelly-roll style, starting with a long side. Place on a lightly greased cookie sheet. Join ends of dough and seal, forming a circle. Cut into ring at 3/4-inch intervals, using a sharp knife or kitchen shears. Cut to within 1-inch of inside of ring. Twist sections to form a petal effect.

Bake 35 minutes or until golden brown. Cool completely.

Combine glaze ingredients. Drizzle over tea ring. Makes 1 large tea ring.

RED RIBBON CRANBERRY COFFEECAKE

....

TOPPING:
1/4 cup flour
2 tablespoons sugar
1 tablespoon butter

BATTER:
2 cups flour
3/4 cup sugar
1 1/2 teaspoons baking powder
1/2 cup butter
1 egg, beaten
1 teaspoon vanilla
3/4 cup milk
1 16-ounce can OCEAN SPRAY®
  jellied cranberry sauce

Preheat oven to 350 degrees. Grease a 9 1/4-inch quiche pan.

Combine topping ingredients in a small mixing bowl. Using a pastry blender or fork, work butter into dry ingredients until butter is the size of small peas. Set aside.

Combine the dry ingredients for the batter in a medium mixing bowl. Using a pastry blender or fork, work butter into dry ingredients (see topping). Combine liquid ingredients in a separate mixing bowl. Add to flour mixture, mixing just until the dry ingredients are moist.

Spread half of the batter into pan. Place cranberry sauce in small bowl and beat with a fork until smooth. Spread over batter. Dollop remaining batter over top. Gently spread with a rubber scraper. Sprinkle topping over coffeecake.

Bake for 20 minutes or until golden brown and a toothpick inserted into the center comes out clean. Makes 1 coffeecake.

THE NEW ENGLAND CRANBERRY SALES CO. FORMED IN 1907 AND SOON MERGED WITH ITS COUNTERPARTS IN NEW JERSEY AND WISCONSIN TO FORM THE AMERICAN CRANBERRY EXCHANGE.

CRANBERRY PUMPKIN BREAD

1 3/4 cups flour
1 cup sugar
2 teaspoons baking powder
1/2 teaspoon baking soda
1 teaspoon cinnamon
1/2 teaspoon nutmeg
1/2 teaspoon allspice
1 cup pumpkin
1/2 cup oil
2 eggs
1 1/2 cups OCEAN SPRAY® fresh or frozen
  cranberries, coarsely chopped

Preheat oven to 350 degrees. Grease and flour an 8 1/2 x 4 1/2 x 2 1/2-inch loaf pan.

Combine dry ingredients in a medium mixing bowl. Combine remaining ingredients, except cranberries, in a separate mixing bowl. Add to dry ingredients, stirring just until dry ingredients are moist. Stir in cranberries.

Spread evenly in loaf pan. Bake 1 1/2 hours or until a toothpick inserted into the center of the bread comes out clean. Remove from pan. Cool completely on a wire rack. Makes 1 loaf.

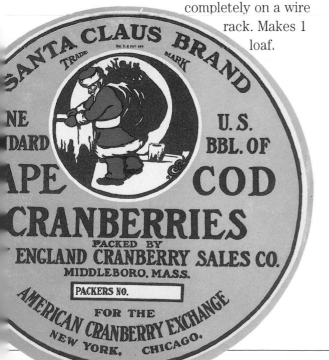

SANTA'S SURPRISE GINGERBREAD MUFFINS

1/2 cup butter or margarine
1/2 cup brown sugar
1/2 cup sugar
1/2 cup molasses
2 eggs
1 teaspoon baking soda
1 cup buttermilk
2 1/4 cups flour
1 1/2 teaspoons cinnamon
3/4 teaspoon ginger
1/4 teaspoon cloves
1/4 teaspoon allspice
1/2 cup CRAN•FRUIT™ cranberry
  raspberry crushed fruit

Preheat oven to 350 degrees. Lightly grease muffin tins.

Using an electric mixer, beat butter, brown sugar and sugar together in a medium mixing bowl until light and fluffy. Add molasses and eggs; mix well.

Add the baking soda to the buttermilk; set aside.

Combine flour, cinnamon, ginger, cloves and allspice in another mixing bowl. Add flour mixture and buttermilk alternately to the butter mixture; mix well after each addition.

Fill each muffin cup halfway with batter. Spoon about 1 teaspoon of crushed fruit into each muffin cup. Top with remaining batter. Bake for about 25 minutes or until golden brown and feel firm to the touch. Remove from tins; cool on a wire rack. Makes 1 dozen muffins.

CHAPTER 9

TEMPTING DESSERTS

A fruit salad. Just a slice of sauce,
grated cheese if desired, with
any salad dressing.

CHOCOLATE DIPPED CRANBERRY COOKIES

1 cup shortening
1 cup sugar
1 teaspoon vanilla
1 egg
2 cups flour
1 teaspoon baking powder
1/2 teaspoon salt
2 cups coarsely chopped OCEAN SPRAY® fresh or frozen cranberries
1 1/3 cups semi-sweet chocolate bits, melted
1 1/4 cups chopped nuts

Preheat oven to 350 degrees. Grease cookie sheets.

Using an electric mixer, beat shortening and sugar together in a medium mixing bowl until light and fluffy. Add vanilla and egg; mix well.

Combine flour, baking powder and salt in a separate mixing bowl. Add to shortening mixture, mixing until a soft dough forms. Stir in cranberries.

IMMEDIATELY drop dough by rounded teaspoonfuls onto cookie sheets. Bake for 10-12 minutes or until golden brown. Transfer cookies to a wire rack; cool completely.

Dip half of each cookie into melted chocolate and then in nuts. Allow chocolate to dry completely. Makes about 3 dozen.

PRECEDING: (LEFT TO RIGHT) CRANBERRY BARS, CHOCOLATE DIPPED CRANBERRY COOKIES AND CRANBERRY THUMBPRINTS.

CRANBERRY THUMBPRINTS

1 20-ounce package refrigerated sugar cookie dough
1 cup CRAN•FRUIT™ crushed fruit, drained
1/2 cup powdered sugar
1 tablespoon water

Preheat oven to 350 degrees.

Roll dough between hands to form 24 1-inch balls. Place on cookie sheets. Press thumb into the center of each ball. Place 1 scant teaspoon crushed fruit in the indent of each cookie.

Bake 7-11 minutes or until lightly golden brown. Cool slightly before transferring to a rack.

Combine powdered sugar and water. Drizzle on each cookie. Makes 2 dozen.

CRANBERRY BROWNIES

1 cup sugar
1/2 cup oil
2 eggs
2 teaspoons vanilla
1/2 cup flour
1/2 cup unsweetened cocoa powder
1 teaspoon baking powder
1 1/2 cups CRAISINS® sweetened dried cranberries

Preheat oven to 350 degrees. Grease and flour an 8-inch square baking pan.

Place sugar, oil, eggs and vanilla in a medium mixing bowl. Thoroughly combine using an electric mixer on medium speed. Add flour, cocoa and baking powder. Mix on low speed for about 1 minute, gradually increasing to medium speed, until thoroughly combined. Add cranberries; mix well.

Spread batter evenly in pan. Bake for 25 minutes or until a toothpick inserted into the center comes out clean. Cool completely before cutting. Makes 9 brownies.

SPICE COOKIES

1/2 cup butter, softened
2 cups flour, divided
1/4 cup milk, divided
1 cup brown sugar
1 egg
2 teaspoons cinnamon
1 teaspoon baking powder
1/2 teaspoon cloves
1/2 cup chopped walnuts
1 1/2 cups coarsely chopped OCEAN SPRAY®
    fresh or frozen cranberries

Preheat oven to 375 degrees.

Place butter in a medium mixing bowl. Add HALF of the flour, HALF of the milk and all remaining ingredients EXCEPT the cranberries. Thoroughly combine using an electric mixer on medium-high speed. Add remaining flour and milk, as well as cranberries, mixing on low speed.

Drop by rounded teaspoonfuls onto ungreased cookie sheets. Bake for 10 minutes or until golden brown. Makes about 30 cookies.

CHOCOLATE CRANBERRY SURPRISE PIE

1 15-ounce package refrigerated pie crusts
1 3 3/8-ounce package chocolate pudding
1 12-ounce package CRAN•FRUIT™ crushed fruit
Whipped cream
Sliced almonds

Prepare pie crust as directed on package for a single crust pie. Prepare chocolate pudding as directed on package; set aside.

Spread crushed fruit evenly on bottom of crust. Gently spread chocolate pudding in crust. Cover with plastic wrap and chill overnight. Garnish with whipped cream and almonds before serving. Makes 1 pie.

CRANBERRY BARS

1 cup butter or margarine, softened
3/4 cup brown sugar
1 egg
2 1/2 cups flour
1 teaspoon baking powder
1 12-ounce package CRAN•FRUIT™ crushed fruit

Preheat oven to 350 degrees. Grease a 9x9-inch square pan.

Mix butter or margarine and brown sugar in a medium mixing bowl until completely blended. Add egg; mix well.

Combine flour and baking powder in a small mixing bowl. Add to butter mixture, mixing well. Spread half of the dough in the pan. Spread crushed fruit on top. Break remaining dough into small pieces and place on top of crushed fruit. Using the back of a metal spoon, gently press top layer of dough into fruit, letting juice mix in.

Bake 30 minutes or until golden brown. Cool completely. Cut into squares. Makes 16 bars.

OCEAN SPRAY BRAND FRESH CRANBERRIES IN NEW CELLOPHANE PACKAGES. (BAG, CIRCA 1948)

PUMPKIN CRANBERRY COOKIES

1 cup sugar
3/4 cup butter or margarine, softened
1 egg
1 cup pumpkin
1 teaspoon vanilla
2 cups flour
1 teaspoon cinnamon
1 teaspoon baking powder
1/2 teaspoon baking soda
1/2 teaspoon nutmeg
1 1/2 cups OCEAN SPRAY® fresh or frozen cranberries, chopped
3/4 cup chopped walnuts

Preheat oven to 350 degrees.

Using an electric mixer, beat sugar and butter together in a medium mixing bowl until light and fluffy. Add egg; mix well. Add pumpkin and vanilla; mix well.

Combine dry ingredients in a separate mixing bowl. Add to pumpkin mixture, mixing just until moist, using an electric mixer. Stir in cranberries and nuts.

Drop by rounded teaspoonfuls onto ungreased cookie sheets. Bake for 20 minutes or until golden brown. Cool completely. Makes about 3 dozen cookies.

FRUITY MOCHA MOUSSE

4 ounces semi-sweet baking chocolate
2 cups heavy cream
2 tablespoons powdered sugar
1 16-ounce can OCEAN SPRAY® jellied cranberry sauce
1/4 cup corn syrup
1/4 cup coffee flavored liqueur
1/4 cup chocolate chips

Melt chocolate on low heat or microwave for 2 minutes on high; set aside.

Using an electric mixer, whip cream in a medium mixing bowl until stiff peaks form. Gradually add powdered sugar while whipping. Gradually add melted chocolate to whipped cream, mixing on low speed. Spoon into individual dessert dishes. Refrigerate at least one hour before serving.

Combine cranberry sauce, corn syrup, coffee liqueur and chocolate chips in a medium saucepan. Cook over medium heat until smooth, whisking frequently. Cool to room temperature. Serve over mousse. Makes 6–8 servings.

FRUITY MOCHA MOUSSE.

WILD BERRY COBBLER

1 1/2 cups OCEAN SPRAY® fresh or frozen cranberries
3 cups pineapple chunks, drained and cut in half
1 cup frozen blueberries
1 cup brown sugar
1 teaspoon cinnamon
1/4 teaspoon nutmeg
2 cups baking mix
1/2 cup milk
Sugar

Preheat oven to 350 degrees.

Combine cranberries, pineapple, blueberries, brown sugar, cinnamon and nutmeg in a medium mixing bowl. Place in a 3-quart soufflé or casserole dish.

Combine baking mix and milk in a small mixing bowl. Drop spoonfuls of dough on top of the fruit. Sprinkle with a little sugar. Bake for 45 minutes or until dough is golden brown. Serve warm. Makes 6–8 servings.

A real turn-over eaten plain instead of pie, or as a pudding with sauce, hot or cold, or with cream or ice cream.

CRANBERRY RAISIN TART

1 15-ounce package refrigerated pie crusts
1 1/2 cups OCEAN SPRAY® fresh or frozen cranberries
1 cup golden raisins
1/2 cup chopped walnuts
1/2 cup brown sugar
1 teaspoon cinnamon
1/4 teaspoon each: nutmeg, ginger, allspice
1/8 teaspoon ground cloves

Preheat oven to 400 degrees.

Lightly dust one side of bottom crust with flour. Place flour side down on a jelly roll pan. Lightly press out the creases with your fingers. Cut the second crust into 1/2-inch strips using a pastry trimmer or knife. Set aside.

Combine remaining ingredients. Place on bottom crust to within 1 1/2 inches of the pastry. Place the pie crust strips lengthwise and crosswise over the filling. Trim strips that are longer than the bottom crust. Carefully fold the 1 1/2 inches of crust over the filling. Seal the crust by pressing the top of a spoon or fork into folded edges. Bake for 25 minutes or until golden brown. Makes 1 tart.

HOLIDAY TRIFLE

1 18.25-ounce package white cake mix
2 4-ounce packages instant chocolate pudding
2 12-ounce packages CRAN•FRUIT™ cranberry raspberry crushed fruit
3 bananas, sliced
1/4 cup sliced almonds

Prepare cake mix as directed on package using a 13x9-inch pan. Cool thoroughly. Cut cake into 1/2-inch squares. Set aside.

Prepare pudding as directed on package. Set aside.

Spread 1/2 cup pudding on bottom of a 4-quart trifle or glass bowl. Place half of the cake squares into the bowl. Press down gently. Spread 2 cups of pudding on top of the cake. Next, layer bananas neatly over pudding. Spread crushed fruit over bananas. Add the remaining cake squares. Press down gently. Spread the remaining 1 1/2 cups pudding on top of cake and sprinkle with sliced almonds. Makes 8–10 servings.

A fruit salad. Just a slice of sauce, grated cheese if desired, with any salad dressing.

Crush the sauce with a fork for pie filling. Bake with crust or just fill and frost.

CHOCOLATE TRUFFLES

9 ounces semi-sweet chocolate
1/2 cup OCEAN SPRAY® jellied cranberry sauce
2 tablespoons heavy cream
2 tablespoons cocoa
1 1/2 tablespoons powdered sugar

Place chocolate, cranberry sauce and heavy cream in a medium saucepan. Cook over medium-low heat until sauce is smooth, whisking frequently. Remove from heat and pour into a glass or plastic bowl. Cover with plastic wrap. Let sit at room temperature to thicken.

Combine cocoa and 1 1/2 tablespoons powdered sugar on a small plate. Scoop out a rounded teaspoonful of chocolate mixture. Roll in cocoa, coating thoroughly. Dust hands with powdered sugar. Roll truffle in hands to form a 1-inch ball. Continue forming truffles with remaining chocolate mixture. Makes 30 truffles.

CHOCOLATE CRANBERRY CHEESECAKE

1 16-ounce can OCEAN SPRAY® jellied
   cranberry sauce
1/2 cup chocolate chips
2 cups graham cracker crumbs
1/2 cup melted butter
1/4 cup sugar
2 8-ounce packages cream cheese
1 cup powdered sugar
2 eggs
1 teaspoon vanilla

Preheat oven to 350 degrees.

Combine cranberry sauce and chocolate chips in a medium saucepan. Melt over medium heat until smooth, whisking frequently. Set aside.

Combine graham cracker crumbs, butter and sugar in a medium mixing bowl. Place mixture in a 10 x 2 3/4-inch springform pan. Press crumbs on bottom and sides of pan, making sides about 2 inches high. Set aside.

Using an electric mixer, beat cream cheese and powdered sugar together in a medium mixing bowl until light and fluffy. Add eggs and vanilla; mix well.

Reserve 1/3 cup of chocolate sauce. Pour remaining sauce into crust, spreading evenly. Pour cream cheese mixture into pan. Spoon remaining chocolate sauce over cream cheese mixture and gently swirl with a knife.

Bake for 1 hour or until the center is set. Makes 1 cheesecake.

CHOCOLATE AND CRANBERRY TEAM UP TO ADD PIZAZZ TO THIS CHEESECAKE.

CRANBERRY FUDGE

1 1/4 cups OCEAN SPRAY® fresh or frozen
   cranberries
1/2 cup light corn syrup
2 cups chocolate chips
1/2 cup powdered sugar
1/4 cup evaporated milk
1 teaspoon vanilla

Line bottom and sides of 8 x 8-inch pan with plastic wrap. Set aside. Bring cranberries and corn syrup to a boil in a medium saucepan. Boil on high for 5-7 minutes, stirring occasionally until the liquid is reduced to 3 tablespoons. Remove from heat.

Immediately add chocolate chips; stir until completely melted. Add remaining ingredients, stirring vigorously until the mixture is thick and glossy.

Pour into prepared pan. Cover and chill until firm. Cut into 1 1/2-inch squares. Store covered in refrigerator. Makes 25 pieces.

TROPICAL PINK SORBET

6 ounces OCEAN SPRAY® pink grapefruit
   juice cocktail
1 15 1/2-ounce can tropical fruit salad, drained

Place ingredients in a food processor. Process until the mixture is smooth. Pour into a non-metal container. Freeze just until firm, about 2 hours.

Break up into pieces and process in food processor until smooth. Return grapefruit mixture to container and freeze until firm.

Remove from freezer about 10 minutes before serving. Spoon into serving dishes. Makes 6 servings.

GLAZED CRANBERRY APPLE WALNUT FRUITCAKE

- 4 cups all-purpose flour
- 1 teaspoon baking soda
- 1 teaspoon baking powder
- 1/4 teaspoon salt
- 1/2 teaspoon cinnamon
- 1/2 teaspoon nutmeg
- 1 cup butter or margarine, softened
- 1 3/4 cups sugar
- 4 eggs, separated
- 1 1/2 cups CRANAPPLE® cranberry apple juice drink
- 1 12-ounce package chopped, pitted dates
- 2 1/2 cups walnuts, coarsely chopped
- 1/2 cup powdered sugar
- 1 cup CRANAPPLE® cranberry apple juice drink
- 1 tablespoon apple brandy

Preheat oven to 300 degrees. Grease and flour a 10-inch tube pan.

Sift 3 1/2 cups flour, baking soda, baking powder, salt and spices onto waxed paper; set aside.

Using an electric mixer, beat butter, sugar and egg yolks together in a medium mixing bowl until light and fluffy. Add flour mixture alternately with cranberry apple juice drink, beginning and ending with dry ingredients. Beat until batter is smooth.

Toss dates and nuts with remaining 1/2 cup flour. Gently mix into cake batter using a rubber scraper; set aside.

Using an electric mixer, beat egg whites in a medium mixing bowl until stiff peaks form. Gently mix into cake batter, using a rubber scraper, until no streaks remain.

Pour batter into pan. Bake for 1 hour 45 minutes or until a toothpick inserted into the cake comes out clean. Cool 10 minutes. Combine powdered sugar, cranberry apple drink and apple brandy in a small bowl. Remove cake from pan and place on serving dish. Prick top and sides of cake with a fork. Brush glaze all over cake. Refrigerate overnight. Makes 8–10 servings.

POACHED PEARS WITH CHOCOLATE CRANBERRY SAUCE

- 6 cups OCEAN SPRAY® cranberry juice cocktail
- 1 cup sugar
- 6 Bartlett pears, peeled and cored with stems intact
- 1 16-ounce can OCEAN SPRAY® jellied cranberry sauce
- 1/2 cup chocolate chips

Combine cranberry juice cocktail and sugar in a large saucepan. Bring to a boil over high heat. Place pears in pan. Cover and simmer on low heat for 10-15 minutes or until pears are tender when pierced with a fork. Turn pears several times during cooking. Remove from heat. Let cool in liquid at room temperature.

Combine cranberry sauce and chocolate chips in medium saucepan. Melt over medium heat, whisking occasionally until smooth.

Remove pears from liquid; drain. To serve, spoon 1/4 cup of sauce on each serving plate. Place pears on plates. Spoon remaining sauce over tops of pears. Makes 6 servings.

CASHEW CLUSTERS

- 9 ounces semi-sweet chocolate
- 1/2 cup CRAISINS® sweetened dried cranberries
- 1/2 cup cashews

Melt chocolate in a double boiler. Remove from heat and cool slightly. Stir in dried cranberries and nuts. Drop by teaspoonfuls onto a cookie sheet. Let harden at room temperature or chill in refrigerator. Makes about 16 clusters.

RIGHT: POACHED PEARS WITH CHOCOLATE CRANBERRY SAUCE.

DOUBLE CHOCOLATE CRANBERRY MOUSSE PIE

- 1 pint heavy cream
- 2 2-ounce bars white baking bars, broken into pieces
- 1 6-ounce chocolate graham cracker crust
- 1 12-ounce package CRAN•FRUIT™ cranberry raspberry crushed fruit
- 2 ounces chocolate chips

Combine 1/2 cup cream and white baking bars in a medium glass mixing bowl. Microwave for 1 1/2 to 2 minutes on high, stirring once. Remove from microwave and stir until smooth. Let cool completely.

Using an electric mixer, beat 1/2 cup cream in a medium mixing bowl until stiff peaks form. Use a rubber scraper to gently mix in the melted baking bars. Pour into pie crust.

Gently spread crushed fruit over mousse mixture.

Combine 1/4 cup cream and chocolate chips in a medium glass mixing bowl. Microwave for 1 minute on high. Remove from microwave and stir until smooth. Cool completely.

Using the mixer, whip remaining cream in a medium mixing bowl until stiff peaks form. Use a rubber scraper to gently mix in the chocolate. Gently spread over pie. Chill for 2 hours. Makes 1 pie.

Variation: Freeze pie for 4 hours for an "ice cream pie-like" texture.

Time was when the cranberry was not valued more than the common barberry. But people have lived to discover its excellent qualities, and since it is so appreciated for its culinary purposes, there are those willing to pay an almost fabulous price for the berry. . . The wealthy would as soon part with the apple as the cranberry, and it is the rage among the rich, and even those who are not so fortunate. . .

— Benjamin Eastwood, The Cranberry and its Culture, 1856

CRANBERRY ALMOND BISCOTTI

- 2 1/4 cups flour
- 1 cup sugar
- 1 teaspoons baking powder
- 1/2 baking soda
- 1 teaspoons cinnamon
- 1/2 teaspoon nutmeg
- 2 eggs
- 2 egg whites
- 1 tablespoon almond or vanilla extract
- 3/4 cup sliced almonds
- 1 6-ounce package CRAISINS® sweetened dried cranberries

Preheat oven to 325 degrees.

Combine dry ingredients in a medium mixing bowl. Whisk together eggs, egg whites and extract in a separate mixing bowl. Add to dry ingredients, mixing just until moist, using an electric mixer on medium speed. Add dried cranberries and almonds; mix thoroughly.

On a floured surface, divide batter in half. Pat each half into a log approximately 14 inches long and 1 1/2-inch wide. Place on a cookie sheet. Bake for 30 minutes or until firm. Cool on wire rack.

Reduce oven temperature to 300 degrees. Cut biscotti into 1/2-inch slices. Stand biscotti upright on cookie sheet. Bake for an additional 20 minutes. Let cool. Store in a loosely covered container. Makes 2 1/2 dozen.

PEANUT BERRY AND JELLIES

1/2 cup butter or margarine, softened
1/2 cup sugar
1/2 cup brown sugar
1/2 cup peanut butter, smooth or crunchy
1 teaspoon vanilla
1 egg
1 1/2 cups flour
1 teaspoon baking soda
1 12-ounce package CRAN•FRUIT™ cranberry raspberry sauce, drained

Preheat oven to 350 degrees.

Using an electric mixer, beat butter or margarine, sugar and brown sugar in a medium mixing bowl until light and fluffy. Add peanut butter, vanilla and egg; mix well.

Combine flour and baking soda in a separate mixing bowl. Add to peanut butter mixture; mix well.

Roll dough between hands to make 1-inch balls. Place on cookie sheets. Press thumb into the center of each ball. Spoon a scant teaspoon of crushed fruit into the indent of each cookie.

Bake 15 minutes or until slightly firm to the touch. Cool completely. Makes about 3 dozen cookies.

PHYLLO BASKETS WITH CRANBERRY PEAR COMPOTE

COMPOTE:
1 1/2 tablespoons cornstarch
1/4 cup cold water
1 tablespoon butter or margarine
2 medium firm, ripe pears, peeled, cored and cut into 1/2-inch pieces
1/2 teaspoon grated fresh ginger
1 16-ounce can OCEAN SPRAY® whole berry cranberry sauce
1/3 cup chopped walnuts
1 tablespoon brandy
1/2 teaspoon nutmeg

BASKETS:
4 sheets phyllo dough
Butter-flavored cooking spray
Whipped cream, garnish

TO PREPARE THE COMPOTE: Combine cornstarch and water in a small bowl; set aside.

Melt butter or margarine in a medium skillet. Add pears and ginger and cook for 1 minute. Break up cranberry sauce and add to the skillet. Bring mixture to a boil. Add cornstarch mixture. Return to a boil over medium high heat, stirring constantly. Boil for 1 minute or until thick. Remove from heat. Stir in nuts, brandy and nutmeg. Let cool to room temperature.

TO PREPARE BASKETS: Preheat oven to 350 degrees.

Place 1 sheet of phyllo on work surface. Lightly spray with cooking spray. Top with a second sheet of phyllo. Lightly spray with cooking spray. Repeat with remaining sheets of phyllo.

Cut the stack of phyllo in half horizontally and then each half into thirds, making 6 pieces. Press each phyllo square into a 10-ounce oven-proof glass custard cup. Press in center and around sides to mold cup. Corners of phyllo should stick up.

Place cups on cookie sheets. Bake for about 10 minutes or until crisp and golden brown. Remove from custard cups. Cool completely on a wire rack.

Spoon compote into each phyllo basket. Garnish with whipped cream. Makes 6 servings.

CRANBERRY PUMPKIN ROLL

5 eggs, separated
1/2 cup sugar
1/2 cup pumpkin
1/2 cup flour
1/4 cup cornstarch
1 1/2 teaspoons cinnamon
1 teaspoon nutmeg
1/2 teaspoon allspice
2 teaspoons baking powder
3 cups non-dairy whipped topping
1 12-ounce package CRAN•FRUIT™
    cranberry raspberry crushed fruit
Powdered sugar
Paper doily

Preheat oven to 375 degrees.

Using an electric mixer, beat egg whites in a medium mixing bowl until stiff peaks form. Set aside.

Combine egg yolks, sugar and pumpkin in a separate mixing bowl. Add remaining dry ingredients, mixing well. Gently mix egg whites into batter using a rubber scraper until no streaks remain.

Line a jelly roll pan with foil and spray with non-stick vegetable spray. Spread batter evenly in pan. Bake for 12 minutes or until a toothpick inserted into the center of the cake comes out clean.

Liberally sprinkle powdered sugar over a clean kitchen towel. Turn the jelly roll out onto the towel and carefully remove foil. Trim off any crisp edges. Roll the cake up in the towel, jelly roll style. Cool completely.

Unroll the cake. Spread non-dairy whipped topping over cake. Drop teaspoons of crushed fruit over whipped topping. Gently spread with a rubber scraper.

Re-roll cake without towel. Lay doily on roll and sprinkle with powdered sugar. Transfer to serving plate. Makes 10–12 servings.

RAVIOLI COOKIES

DOUGH:
2 cups flour
1 teaspoon salt
2 tablespoons cold water
1 teaspoon vanilla
1 cup cold butter, cut into 1/2-inch cubes

FILLING:
1 1/4 cups crushed pineapple, well drained
3/4 cup OCEAN SPRAY® whole berry
    cranberry sauce
1/2 teaspoon nutmeg
6 tablespoons chopped walnuts

Powdered sugar

TO MAKE DOUGH:
Place flour and salt in a food processor. Add water and vanilla; process until mixed. With processor running, add butter a few cubes at a time. Process until the mixture forms a ball. Wrap in plastic wrap and chill about 1 hour or until firm.

TO MAKE FILLING:
Combine filling ingredients in a small mixing bowl. Set aside.

Preheat oven to 350 degrees.

Break off 2 small pieces of dough. Roll each piece into a 6 x 5-inch rectangle on a lightly floured work surface. On one piece of dough, place rounded 1/2-teaspoonfuls of filling, 2 across and 3 or 4 down and at least 1/2-inch apart. Lightly brush dough around filling with water. Top with second piece of dough, lightly pressing around filling to seal. Cut apart, using a pastry trimmer or knife.

Place on a cookie sheet and repeat with remaining dough and filling.

Bake for 12 minutes or until golden brown. Cool completely on a cooling rack. Lightly dust with powdered sugar. Makes 2 1/2 dozen cookies.

TIRAMISU

CRANBERRY LAYER:
1 12-ounce package OCEAN SPRAY® fresh or
   frozen cranberries, finely chopped
3/4 cup water
3/4 cup sugar
3 tablespoons water

RICOTTA CHEESE LAYER:
1 1/4 cups ricotta cheese
1 cup powdered sugar
1/4 cup fat-free sour cream
1/4 cup coffee liqueur

1 5-ounce bag cream puff cookies, crushed
1/4 cup grated chocolate

TO MAKE CRANBERRY LAYER:
Combine cranberries, 3/4 cup of water and sugar
in a medium saucepan. Bring to a boil; reduce
heat and simmer 10 minutes. Let cool. Stir in 3
tablespoons of water; set aside.

TO MAKE RICOTTA CHEESE LAYER:
Combine ricotta cheese, powdered sugar, sour
cream and coffee liqueur in a medium mixing
bowl, mixing well.

TO LAYER DESSERT.
Spoon 2 tablespoons of the cranberry mixture in a
medium wine glass. Add 1/3 cup cookie crumbs,
spreading to the edge of the glass. Spoon 1/4 cup
of the ricotta mixture over the crumbs.

Continue layering by adding 1/3 cup cookie
crumbs and 1/4 cup cranberry mixture. Finish
with 1/4 cup of the ricotta mixture.

Repeat the layering process with remaining
ingredients in 3 additional medium wine glasses.
Amounts needed in layering will vary with size
and shape of wine glasses.

Top each tiramisu with grated chocolate. Let
chill 6 hours before serving. Makes 4 servings.

CHOCOLATE PÂTÉ WITH CRANBERRY COULIS

COULIS:
1 1/2 cups OCEAN SPRAY® jellied cranberry
   sauce
3/4 cup OCEAN SPRAY® cranberry juice cocktail
1 teaspoon lime juice

PÂTÉ:
1 1/2 cups heavy cream
1 egg yolk
12 ounces semi-sweet chocolate
1/3 cup corn syrup
1/4 cup butter or margarine
1 teaspoon vanilla
Whipped cream, garnish

TO MAKE CRANBERRY COULIS:
Puree all ingredients in a blender or food processor until smooth. Chill. Makes 1 3/4 cups.

TO MAKE PÂTÉ:
Line an 8 1/2 x 4 1/2 x 2 1/2 inch loaf pan with
plastic wrap. Combine 1/4 cup cream with egg
yolk; set aside.

Combine chocolate, corn syrup and butter or
margarine in a medium saucepan. Cook over low
heat until melted, stirring frequently. Remove
from heat. Add cream mixture to saucepan. Cook
1 minute over medium heat, stirring constantly.
Transfer chocolate to a large mixing bowl and let
cool to room temperature.

Beat remaining cream with vanilla in a small
mixing bowl until soft peaks form. Use a rubber
scraper to gently mix the chocolate into the
whipped cream. Pour into pan. Cover with plastic
wrap. Refrigerate overnight or freeze 3 hours.

TO SERVE:
Spoon some Cranberry Coulis on a dessert plate.
Place a slice of Chocolate Pâté on plate. Garnish
with whipped cream. Makes 10 servings.

BLUSHING PEACH BUNDLES

Heavy duty aluminum foil
6 firm, ripe peaches or
   nectarines, each cut into
   8 wedges
1 1/2 cups CRAN•RASP-
   BERRY® raspberry
   cranberry juice drink
1/4 cup raspberry preserves
1 teaspoon nutmeg
1 1/2 tablespoons cornstarch
Vanilla ice cream

Cut six 12 x 14 5/16-inch pieces of aluminum foil. Place 8 peach or nectarine wedges on each sheet of foil. Fold up sides of foil to form a cup.

Combine juice drink, preserves and nutmeg. Add cornstarch; mix well. Pour about 1/3 cup of the juice mixture into each cup; twist foil to seal.

Place bundles on grill and cook over medium heat. Swirl bundles occasionally to stir sauce. Cook 12-15 minutes or until sauce has thickened.

Carefully open bundles, and let fruit cool slightly. Serve in foil cups topped with vanilla ice cream. Makes 6 servings.

CHOCOLATE JEWEL COOKIES

1 cup butter, softened
1 cup sugar
1 egg
1 teaspoon vanilla
2 1/4 cups flour
1/4 cup cocoa
1 teaspoon baking powder
1 12-ounce package
   CRAN•FRUIT™ crushed
   fruit, drained

Using an electric mixer, beat butter and sugar together in a medium mixing bowl until light and fluffy. Add egg and vanilla; mix well. Combine dry ingredients in a separate mixing bowl. Add to butter mixture, mixing well.

Roll dough between hands to form 1-inch balls. Place on ungreased cookie sheets. Press thumb into the center of each ball. Place 1/2-rounded teaspoon crushed fruit in the indent of each cookie.

Bake about 13 minutes or until slightly firm to the touch. Makes 3 1/2 dozen cookies.

OATMEAL CRANBERRY CHOCOLATE CHUNK COOKIES

2/3 cup butter or margarine,
   softened
2/3 cup brown sugar
2 eggs
1 1/2 cups old-fashioned oats
1 1/2 cups flour
1 teaspoon baking soda
1/2 teaspoon salt
1 6-ounce package
   CRAISINS® sweetened
   dried cranberries
2/3 cup white chocolate
   chunks or chips

Preheat oven to 375 degrees.

Using an electric mixer, beat butter or margarine and sugar together in a medium mixing bowl until light and fluffy. Add eggs, mixing well. Combine oats, flour, salt and baking soda in a separate mixing bowl. Add to butter mixture in several additions, mixing well after each addition. Stir in dried cranberries and white chocolate chunks.

Drop by rounded teaspoonfuls onto ungreased cookie sheets. Bake for 10-12 minutes or until golden brown. Makes 2 1/2 dozen.

CHRISTMAS CAPPUCCINO CAKE WITH CRANBERRY DRIZZLE

1 14.5 or 16 ounce package angel food cake mix
5 rounded tablespoons cappuccino-flavored instant coffee
2 tablespoons butter or margarine
1/4 cup cappuccino flavored instant coffee
1 16-ounce can OCEAN SPRAY® jellied cranberry sauce

Prepare cake mix as directed on package, adding the 5 tablespoons instant coffee gradually after batter has been mixed. Bake and cool as directed.

Melt butter with instant coffee in a small saucepan. Add cranberry sauce. Cook over medium low heat, whisking constantly, until sauce is melted and smooth. Cool to room temperature.

Drizzle some sauce on plate. Top with a slice of cake. Makes 12 servings.

COUNTRY CRANBERRY RHUBARB TART

1 16-ounce can OCEAN SPRAY® whole berry cranberry sauce
1/3 cup sugar
1 1/2 tablespoons cornstarch
3/4 pound rhubarb stalks, cut into 1/2-inch pieces
Pastry for a 9-inch single crust pie
Powdered sugar

Preheat oven to 375 degrees.

Combine cranberry sauce, sugar and cornstarch in a medium mixing bowl. Stir in rhubarb. Pour into a pastry-lined 9-inch pie plate. Fold crust edge over the filling, pleating to fit.

Bake for 40 minutes or until golden brown. Cool completely. Sprinkle with powdered sugar before serving. Makes 1 tart.

"The Indians and English use them much, boyling them with Sugar for Sauce to eat with their meat; and it is a delicate Sauce, especially with Roasted Mutton: some make tarts with them as with Goose Berries."

—John Josselyn, New England's Rarities, 1672

CRANBERRY BREAD PUDDING

6 cups toasted whole wheat bread cubes, packed
1 cup OCEAN SPRAY® fresh or frozen cranberries
2 cups CRAN•RASPBERRY® raspberry cranberry juice drink
1 cup honey
1/2 cup butter
1 teaspoon cinnamon
1/2 teaspoon nutmeg
1 cup raisins

Preheat oven to 350 degrees. Grease a 2-quart casserole dish or pudding pan.

Pour bread cubes into prepared pan. Set aside.

Combine all ingredients in a large saucepan. Bring to a boil over medium heat. Boil gently just until the cranberries begin to pop. Pour cranberry mixture over bread cubes. Let sit 15 minutes.

Bake pudding for 45 minutes. Serve warm with vanilla ice cream. Makes 10 servings.

CHAPTER 10

JUST FOR KIDS

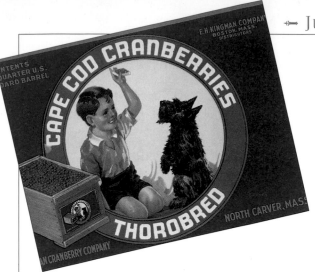

SUMMER SLUSH

3 cups CRANAPPLE® cranberry apple juice drink
1 cup orange juice
Club soda

Stir together cranberry apple drink and orange juice in a large glass bowl. Freeze until mixture is of slush consistency. Scoop out 3/4 cup of slush into a glass. Top with a splash of club soda. Makes about 6 servings.

STRAWBERRY FROSTY FREEZE

3 ounces CRAN•STRAWBERRY™ cranberry strawberry juice drink
2 ounces thawed frozen strawberries
3/4 ounce grenadine
1 cup crushed ice
Strawberry, garnish

Put all ingredients, except garnish, in a blender. Blend on high speed for a few seconds or until ingredients are thoroughly combined. Garnish with strawberry. Makes 1 serving.

PRECEDING: (LEFT TO RIGHT) GRAPE APE, STRAWBERRY FROSTY FREEZE, ROCKIN' RHINO (PAGE 109), CHOCOLATE CHIMP.

KOOL KOALA

8 ounces CRAN•GRAPE® grape cranberry juice drink
1/2 ounce cherry juice
Lemon-lime soda
Cherry, garnish

Put grape cranberry drink and cherry juice in a blender. Blend for a few seconds on high speed. Pour into a tall glass with crushed ice. Top with soda. Garnish with a cherry. Makes 1 serving.

GRAPE APE

8 ounces CRAN•GRAPE® grape cranberry juice drink
1/2 cup vanilla ice cream, softened
8 ounces club soda

Put grape cranberry drink and ice cream in a blender. Blend on high speed for a few seconds or until ingredients are thoroughly combined. Stir in club soda. Makes 2 servings.

CHOCOLATE CHIMP

8 ounces CRAN•RASPBERRY® raspberry cranberry juice drink
2 ounces half-and-half
1 ounce chocolate syrup
Whipped cream, garnish
Chocolate sprinkles, garnish
Milk chocolate piece, garnish

Put raspberry cranberry drink, half-and-half and chocolate syrup into a blender. Blend on high speed for a few seconds or until ingredients are thoroughly combined. Garnish with whipped cream, chocolate sprinkles and milk chocolate piece. Makes 1 serving.

ROCKIN' RHINO

8 ounces CRAN•STRAWBERRY™ cranberry
  strawberry juice drink
2 ounces strawberries
Lemon-lime soda
Whipped cream, garnish
Cherry or strawberry, garnish

Put cranberry strawberry drink and strawberries in a blender. Blend on high speed for a few seconds or until ingredients are thoroughly combined. Pour into a tall glass with crushed ice. Top with soda. Garnish with whipped cream and a cherry or strawberry. Makes 1 serving.

AWESOME ALLIGATOR

8 ounces CRAN•STRAWBERRY™ cranberry
  strawberry juice drink
3/4 ounce cream of coconut
Dash grenadine syrup
Club soda, optional
Whipped cream, garnish
Cherry or strawberry, garnish

Put all ingredients, except club soda and garnishes, in a blender. Blend for a few seconds on high speed or until ingredients are thoroughly combined. Pour into a tall glass with crushed ice. Top with club soda, if desired. Garnish with whipped cream and a
cherry or strawberry.
Makes 1 serving.

*SUITSUS BRAND WAS DISTRIBUTED
BY BOSTON'S COLLEY CRANBERRY
COMPANY.*

PURPLE PARROT

8 ounces CRAN•GRAPE® grape cranberry juice
  drink
1 ounce cream of coconut
Lemon-lime soda
Whipped cream, garnish

Put grape cranberry drink and cream of coconut in a blender. Blend for a few seconds on high speed or until ingredients are thoroughly combined. Pour into a tall glass with crushed ice. Top with soda. Garnish with whipped cream. Makes 1 serving.

COOKIE COOLER

8 ounces CRAN•RASPBERRY® raspberry
  cranberry juice drink
3 chocolate sandwich cookies
2 scoops vanilla ice cream
Whipped cream, garnish
Chocolate sandwich cookie, garnish

Put all ingredients, except garnishes, in a blender. Blend for a few seconds on high speed or until ingredients are thoroughly combined. Garnish with whipped cream and cookie. Makes 1 serving.